# THE PRICE
# OF GOD'S MIRACLE
# WORKING POWER

# THE PRICE
# OF GOD'S MIRACLE
# WORKING POWER

By

## A.A. Allen

Printed in the United States of America and Australia.

Bottom of the Hill Publishing

Memphis, TN

www.BottomoftheHillPublishing.com

ISBN: 978-1-61203-494-2

# Content

# CHAPTER 1

## THE PRICE OF GOD'S MIRACLE WORKING POWER

How long had I been here in this closet? Days or just hours? Surely it seemed days since at my own request I had heard my wife lock that closet door from the outside! What would she think about me shutting myself away for so long? Had it really been days or just hours? Was I really getting anywhere with God? Would God answer? Would God satisfy that hunger of my soul or would I have to admit defeat again as so often I had done? No! I'd stay right here on my knees until God answered, or I would die in the attempt! Hadn't God's word said, "They that wait upon the Lord shall renew their strength, they shall mount up-up-UP-with wings-with wings as eagles; they shall run and not be weary; they shall ---."

Had my wife opened the door? No, it was still closed! But the light, where was the light coming from? It was then that I began to realize that the light that was filling my prayer closet was God's glory! It wasn't the closet door that had opened, but rather the door of heaven instead!

The presence of God was so real and powerful that I felt I would die right there on my knees. It seemed that if God came any closer, I could not stand it! Yet I wanted it and was determined to have it. Little wonder that Paul under like circumstance, "fell to the earth". Acts 9:4. No wonder John, "fell at his feet as dead". Rev. 1:17.

Was this the answer? Was God going to speak to me? Would God at last, after these many years, satisfy my longing heart? I seemed to lose consciousness of everything but the mighty presence of God. I trembled, I tried to see Him and then was afraid that I would, for suddenly I realized that should I see Him, I would die. Just His glorious presence was enough!

Then like a whirlwind, I heard His voice. It was God! He was speaking to me! This was the glorious answer that I had sought so diligently and for which I had waited so long. Yes, this was what I had been waiting for since my conversion at the age of twenty-three. Yes, this was what my longing soul had cried for ever since God called me to the ministry.

That call to the ministry had come with such force and was so definite that nothing could ever make me doubt it. From the time of my conversion God had made it so real to me even though my past life had not been spent in such a way as to provide any preparation for this work.

From the time of my conversion, I realized my need of much study if ever I were to fulfill the call of God upon my life. Therefore, I spent many hours reading the Bible, and seeking to understand its message and meaning. To my simple untaught soul, God seemed to mean exactly what he said -- and seemed to say it directly to me through His Word -- "As ye go, preach, saying, The kingdom of heaven is at hand. HEAL THE SICK, cleanse the lepers, raise the dead, cast out devils: freely ye have received, freely give." Matt. 10:7. All this seemed included in a call to the ministry, yet I DID NOT SEE IT BEING DONE! I was myself powerless to carry out these commands of Christ. Yet I knew that it COULD BE DONE, for Christ would not give a command which could not be carried out!

Before my conversion, I knew so little about God and his word, that I could not even quote John 3:16, nor name the four gospels. In the Methodist church where I was converted and of which I became a member, I was not taught to expect to be baptized with the Holy Ghost as the first disciples were on the day of Pentecost, nor to expect the signs mentioned in Mark 16:17,18 to follow me as a believer in the Lord. I was taught to believe on the Lord Jesus Christ for salvation, and was gloriously saved, and set free from condemnation for sin. Then as I searched the Scriptures, asking God to lead me to those readings from which I would receive the greatest benefit, the Lord began to reveal to me the truths of the baptism of the Holy Ghost, the signs following, the gifts of the spirit, and the supernatural things of God.

It was not long until God led me into a Pentecostal church, where I began to see in a small measure the blessings of

God, and a few of the manifestations of the Spirit. It was in these meetings that I became convinced that I needed the Baptism with the Spirit, and there I began to pray and earnestly seek God for that experience.

Thirty days after my conversion, I was gloriously filled with the Holy Ghost, in an Assembly of God camp meeting in Miami, Oklahoma, speaking in other tongues as the Spirit gave utterance.

I had read, "Ye shall receive power after that the Holy Ghost is come upon you." Acts 1:8. I fully expected that with the infilling of the Holy Ghost, I would immediately have power to heal the sick, and to perform miracles. It did not take me long to realize that more was required than the baptism with the Holy Ghost, in order to consistently see these results. The baptism with the Spirit provides access to this power, but the gifts of the Spirit provide the channels through which this power operates. I began immediately to pray and seek the gifts of the Spirit. I felt I must have power to heal the sick, for I knew that God never called anyone to preach the Gospel without commissioning him also to heal the sick.

The power of the Holy Ghost may be readily likened to the power of electricity. When one is filled with the Spirit, it is as though he has had his house wired, and established connection with the "power house". Many people use electricity for years just to provide light! They never take advantage of the great possibilities that are available through using the appliances which electricity will operate. The gifts of the Spirit may be likened to the appliances. As new gifts are added more work can be done, with greater ease. The power has not changed, but it is made more effective. God never intended to STOP when he had filled his people with the Spirit. This is just the beginning. "Covet earnestly the best gifts." I Cor. 12:31. This, I found, is the path to greater accomplishment for God.

Two years after my conversion, I was happily married, and began my ministry.

For more than a year, my wife and I continued preaching this glorious gospel of salvation, the baptism with the Spirit, the second coming of Christ, and DIVINE HEALING. In every revival meeting, I always planned at least two nights in each week to be set aside for preaching divine healing, and prayer for the sick. During this time, we saw a large number of miraculous healings, for God honored the preaching of His word. But I knew that God's plan included greater things for me, and I believed that there would be a time in the future when they would be a reality in my life.

Many times, my wife and I would search the scriptures together, becoming more convinced as we did so that God's promises concerning the signs following, the gifts of the Spirit, healings, and miracles were meant for us, today. It was also plain to see that we did not possess that power in the fullness that God had promised. We knew there must be a scriptural reason why we were so lacking in power. Since God cannot lie, the fault had to be WITHIN OURSELVES!

It was while pastoring my first church, an Assembly of God church in Colorado, that I definitely made up my mind that I MUST hear from heaven, and know the reason that my ministry was not confirmed by signs and wonders.

I felt sure that if I would fast and pray, God would in some way speak to me, and reveal to me what stood between me and the miracle-working power of God in my ministry. I was so hungry for the power of God in my own life that I felt I could not stand in my pulpit, nor even preach again, until I had heard from God, and told my wife that this was my plan.

It was then that I had the greatest battle of my life. Satan was determined that I should NOT fast and pray until God answered. Many times he whipped me or tricked me out of that prayer closet. Satan knew that if I ever actually contacted God, there would be much damage to his kingdom, and he meant to do all in his power to hinder me from making that contact.

Day after day, I went into the prayer closet, determined to stay until God had spoken to me. Again and again, I came out without the answer.

Again and again my wife would say to me, "I thought you said this was the time you were going to stay until you got the answer." Then she would smile in her own sweet way, remembering that "the spirit indeed is willing, BUT THE FLESH IS WEAK!"

Again and again I answered her, "Honey, I really meant to pray it through this time, but -- !" It seemed there was always a reason why I couldn't stay in that closet until the answer came. I always justified myself by saying I would pray it through tomorrow. Things would be more favorable then.

The Lord encouraged my heard by calling to my attention how Daniel held on in fasting and prayer, and wrested the answer from the hands of Satan, although it took three weeks to do so. (See Daniel 10:1 and 12)

The next day found me on my knees in the closet again. I had told my wife I would never come out until I heard from God. I REALLY THOUGHT I MEANT IT.

But a few hours later, when I began to smell the odor of food that my wife was preparing for herself and our small son, I was soon out of the closet and in the kitchen, inquiring, "What smells so delicious, dear?"

A few moments later, while I was at the table, God spoke to my heart. I had only taken one bite of food, and I stopped. God had spoken to me. I knew that until I wanted to hear from God MORE THAN ANYTHING ELSE IN THE WORLD, more than food, more than the gratification of the flesh, GOD WOULD NEVER GIVE ME THE ANSWER TO THE QUESTION THAT WAS IN MY HEART!

I arose quickly from the table, and said to my wife, "Honey, I mean business with God this time! I'm going back into that closet, and I want you to lock me inside. I am going to stay there until I hear from God."

"Oh," she replied, "you'll be knocking for me to open the door in an hour or so." She knew that so many times I had said THIS was the time I would stay until I had the answer, she was beginning to wonder if I really could subdue the flesh long enough to defeat the devil. Nevertheless, I heard her lock the door from the outside. Before she left, she said, "I'll let you out any time you knock."

I answered, "I'll not knock until I have the answer that I have wanted so long." At last I had definitely made up my mind to stay there till I heard from God, no matter what the cost!

Hour after hour, I battled with the devil and the flesh in that closet! Many were the times I almost gave up. It seemed to me that days were slipping by, and my progress was so slow! Many times I was tempted to give it all up, and try to be satisfied without the answer -- to go on just as I had been doing. But deep in my soul I knew I could never be satisfied to do that. I had tried it, and found that it was not enough.

No! I would stay right here on my knees until God answered, or I would die in the attempt! Then the glory of God began to fill the closet. I thought for a moment that my wife had opened the door, as the closet door began to grow light. But my wife had not opened the door of the closet -- JESUS HAD OPENED THE DOOR OF HEAVEN, and the closet was flooded with light, the light of the glory of God!

I do not know how long I had stayed in the closet before this happened, but it doesn't matter. I do not care to know. I only know I prayed UNTIL!

The presence of God was so real, so wonderful, and so powerful that I felt I would die right there on my knees. It seemed that if God came any closer, I could not stand it! Yet I wanted it, and was determined to have it.

Was this my answer? Was God going to speak to me? Would God, at last, after these many years, satisfy my longing heart? How long had I been here? I didn't know! I seemed to lose consciousness of everything but the mighty presence of God. I tried to see Him, and then was afraid that I would, for suddenly I realized that should I seem Him, I would die. (Exodus 33:20.) Just His glorious presence was enough!

If only He would speak to me now! If He would just answer my one question, "Lord, why can't I heal the sick? Why can't I work miracles in Your name? Why do signs not follow my ministry as they did that of Peter, John and Paul?"

Then like a whirlwind, I heard His voice! It was God! He was speaking to me! This was the glorious answer for which I had waited so long!

In His presence I felt like one of the small pebbles at the foot of the towering Rockies. I felt I was unworthy even to hear His voice. But He wasn't speaking to me because I was worthy. He was speaking to me because I was needy. Centuries ago, He had promised to supply that need. This was the fulfillment of that promise.

It seemed that faster than any human could possibly speak faster than I could follow mentally, God was talking to me. My heart cried out, "Speak a little more slowly. I want to remember it all!"

It seemed God was speaking to me so fast, and of so many things I could never remember it all. Yet I knew I could never forget! God was giving me a list of the things which stood between me and the power of God. After each new requirement was added to the list in my mind, there followed a brief explanation, or sermonette, explaining that requirement and its importance.

Some of the things God spoke to me sounded like scriptures. I knew some of them were, but those first three -- could they be from the Bible?

If I had known there were so many things to remember, I would have brought a pencil and paper! I hadn't expected that God would speak in such a definite way, and give me such a long list. I had never dreamed that I was falling so far short of the glory of God. I hadn't realized there were so many things in my life that generated doubt and hindered my faith.

While God continued to speak to me, I began to feel in my pockets for a pencil. At last I located a short one, but the lead was broken. Quickly I sharpened it with my teeth. I searched for a piece of paper. I couldn't find any. Suddenly I remembered the cardboard box filled with winter clothes which I was using for an altar. I would write on the box.

Now I was ready!

I asked the Lord to please start all over again at the beginning, and let me write the things down one at a time -- to speak slowly enough so that I could get it all on paper.

Once more God started at the first, and spoke to me one after another the many things He had already mentioned. As God spoke to me, I wrote them down.

When the last requirement was written down on the list, God spoke once again, and said, "This is the answer. When you have placed on the altar of consecration and obedience the last thing on your list, YE SHALL NOT ONLY HEAL THE SICK, BUT IN MY NAME SHALL YE CAST OUT DEVILS. YE SHALL SEE MIGHTY MIRACLES AS IN MY NAME YE PREACH THE WORD, FOR BEHOLD, I GIVE YOU POWER OVER ALL THE POWER OF THE ENEMY."

God revealed to me at the same time that the things that were hindrances to my ministry, and had prevented God from working with me, confirming the Word with signs following, were the very same things which were hindering so many thousands of others.

Now it began to grow darker in the closet. I felt His mighty power begin to lift. For a few more moments, His presence lingered, and then I was alone.

Alone, yet not alone.

I trembled under the mighty lingering presence of God. I fumbled at the bottom of the cardboard box on which I had been writing. In the dark, I tore the part on which I had written from the box. In my hand I held the list. At last, here was the price I must pay for the power of God in my life and ministry. THE PRICE TAG FOR THE MIRACLE-WORKING POWER OF GOD!

Frantically, I pounded on the locked door. Again and again I pounded. At last, I heard my wife coming. She opened the door. The moment she saw me, she knew I had been with God. Her first words were, "You've got the answer!"

"Yes, honey. God has paid me a visit from heaven, and here is the answer."

In my hand was the old brown piece of cardboard, with the answer that had cost so many hours of fasting and prayer and waiting, and -- yes -- believing!

My wife and I sat down at the table with the list before us, and as I told her the story, we both wept, as together we went down the list.

There were thirteen items on the list when I came out of the closet, but I erased the last two before showing the list to my wife, because those two were so personal that even my wife shall never know what they were. She has never asked, for she realizes that these things MUST remain between me and God.

The remaining eleven things make up the contents of this book. There is one entire chapter devoted to each of these eleven requirements. If you, too, have longed for the manifestation of the mighty power of God in your own life and ministry, I trust that these thoughts shall inspire you, and that God may speak to you, as he did me, and lead you on to new victory and greater usefulness because of this book.

Since God spoke to me that day in the closet, many pages have been torn from the calendar. In fact, many calendars have been replaced by new ones. As the time has passed, one by one, I have marked the requirements from my list. The list grew smaller and smaller, as I shouted the victory over Satan, and marked off one after another!

Finally, I was down to the last two. Satan said to me,

"You've marked off eleven items, but here are two you'll never mark off. I've got you whipped."

But by the grace of God, I told the devil he was a liar. If God said I could mark them all off, He would help me to do it!

Yet, it seemed I would never be able to mark off the last two.

Never will I forget the day I looked over my list, and found, praise God, there was only one thing left! If I could mark that off, I could claim the promise that God had made to me.

I had to claim that promise! Millions were sick and afflicted, beyond the help of medical science. Someone MUST bring deliverance to them. God had called me to take deliverance to the people. GOD HAS CALLED EVERY MINISTER OF THE GOSPEL TO DO THE SAME! (Ezek. 34:1-4.)

Many have been the times when God has poured out His Spirit in my meetings in a measure, as I have traveled across the states. However, I knew that when I marked the last item from my list, I would see such miracles as I had never seen before. In the meantime, I would patiently strive toward victory, trusting God to help me until victory came. Trusting that when that victory was mine, God would be glorified, and others, too, would be encouraged to seek God for his power.

At this writing, I am conducting a "BACK TO GOD HEALING REVIVAL" at Calvary Temple in Oakland, California. Many say it is the greatest REVIVAL in the history of Oakland. Hundreds say that they have never witnessed such a dynamic moving of the power of God. The meeting is now in its fifth great week. From the growing interest and increasing attendance the meeting could, no doubt, continue indefinitely.

Night after night, the waves of Divine Glory so sweep over the congregation that many testify of being healed while sitting in their seats. Again and again as we have felt the mighty power of God settling over the meeting, people have risen to their feet to testify of instant healings, some of which are visibly miraculous, such as outward tumors disappearing, the crippled made whole.

I have felt goiters disappear at the touch of my hand in Jesus' name!

The shouts of victory are many as the blind see. One woman testified, "It was like coming out of the dark into the sunlight."

We prayed for a woman with throat trouble. After a few moments, she was seen hurrying to the ladies rest room. After returning to the auditorium, she testified that after prayer, something came loose out of her throat and came up into her mouth. she had hurried to the rest room to dispose of it. It was some kind of foreign growth (doubtless cancer) -- whitish orange in color.

Ruptures as large as a person's fist have disappeared overnight. Cancer, deafness, tumors, goiters, sugar diabetes, every known disease and many unknown, disappear, as in the name of Jesus, we lay hands upon the sick. Genuine healings are proven in many cases by doctors' statements and x-rays.

We stand in holy awe, and marvel at the miracle working power of God, as it has moved night after night from the very beginning of this meeting. Hundreds have been delivered from the power of the enemy -- saved, healed, or filled with the Spirit.

In this meeting, it has been impossible to have what is generally termed a "healing line". At least ninety percent of those upon whom we have laid hands are prostrated under the mighty power of God immediately. Some dance a few steps, or weave drunkenly under the power of the Spirit before falling. (See Jer. 23:9). Under these circumstances, it is impossible to have people march on after prayer.

This is the mighty power of God moving upon the people. It is the same power that caused John to "fall at his feet as dead". (Rev. 1:17.)

Many say that the most outstanding thing about this meeting is that such a large percentage of the sick are receiving such miraculous deliverance. It would be a conservative estimate to say that at least ninety percent, or even more of those prayed for have been marvelously healed.

Tonight's service was designated "Holy Ghost Night." Calvary Temple was packed to the doors, with people sitting on the altar benches. (This is being written at 2:00 am after a great Holy Ghost service.) Eternity alone will reveal the number of people who were filled or refilled with the Spirit. We had announced that in this service, hands would be laid upon seekers for the infilling of the Spirit, according to Acts 8:17. After the sermon, all who had not already been filled during the service came down the outside aisle in a line. With only a few exceptions, everyone we touched in the name of Jesus fell prostrate. What an unusual sight to stand on the platform afterwards, and look upon the many "slain of the Lord" in every available altar space, and even down the aisles! Sweeter yet, the sound of the heavenly music of voices raised in united praise to God, as the Spirit filled obedient believers, and they began to speak in new tongues and magnify God. (Mark 16:17; Acts 10:46)

I do not claim to possess a single gift of the Spirit, nor to have power to impart any gift to others, yet all the gifts of the Spirit are in operation, night after night.

Many are exercising the gifts of the Spirit WITHOUT IMPOSITION OF HANDS OR PROPHETIC UTTERANCE!

God is confirming His Word WITH SIGNS FOLLOWING!

Why have I seen such a change in the results of my ministry? You ask WHY? Have you not guessed?

THE LAST ITEM OF THE LIST GOD GAVE TO ME in the closet of prayer HAS BEEN MARKED OFF THE LIST AT LAST! Hallelujah! Many times, I almost gave up hope of ever being able to mark that last one off, but at last it is gone! By God's grace, GONE FOREVER!

With the marking off of the last requirement on my list, has come the fulfillment of God's promise. THE SICK ARE HEALED. DEVILS ARE CAST OUT. MIGHTY MIRACLES ARE SEEN IN THE NAME OF JESUS, AS HIS WORD IS PREACHED!

The chapters which follow give the requirements which God gave to me, and are dedicated to all those who are hungry for the MIRACLE WORKING POWER OF GOD.

# CHAPTER 2

## "THE DISCIPLE IS NOT ABOVE HIS MASTER, NOR THE SERVANT ABOVE HIS LORD"

What strange words! Why should God speak thus to me?

Somehow, I knew that I had read those words somewhere, but where? (I later discovered that this was quoted from the Bible -- Matt. 10:24.) But this was the voice of God, speaking directly to ME. This was the same voice which had spoken to Phillip (Acts 8:30), saying, "Go near, and join thyself to this chariot." It was the voice which Peter had heard (Acts 10:15), saying, "What God hath cleansed that call not thou common." The voice which God's Word tells us may still be heard today. "As the Holy Ghost saith, today if ye will hear his voice harden not your hearts, as in the provocation, in the day of temptation in the wilderness." Heb. 3:7, 8. Now I was hearing the voice of God. All others who might share in the message of these words were for the moment blotted out of my thinking. I had asked God for a solution to my problem, and God was giving the answer.

First of all, I must know that NEVER could there be any possibility of being above my Master, Jesus.

You say, "What is so strange about that? Surely no one would expect to be above HIM!

But wait! You may find that you too, just as I had, have been seeking and expecting that very thing. I had read His promise, "He that believeth on me, the works that I do shall he do also; and greater works than these shall he do; because I go unto my Father." John 14:12. Although it seemed hardly reasonable that anyone could really do a greater miracle than those done by Jesus, yet this seemed to be what the scripture said. Many times I had wondered about the meaning of this scripture. The thought that the disciple could do a greater miracle than his Lord seemed to be a direct contradiction of the spirit of the scripture.

Now I could see that this promise, like all God's promises, is true when rightly understood. "Greater works shall he do," in the sense that Jesus was only one, limited by time and transportation difficulties to a small area and a few people. Those who believe on Him are many. They are scattered over the face of the entire earth. Many of His modern disciples have circled the globe, preaching to thousands at one time by means of electrical amplification systems, and to vast unseen audiences through radio and television, bringing deliverance to greater multitudes than did Jesus. Where Jesus reached hundreds, His followers are reaching thousands. The works of power which are done today are THE SAME WORKS which He did -- greater in quantity, but not in quality. EVERY BELIEVER has promised to him the same power which Jesus used -- miracles after the same pattern which they saw their Master do, first in the flesh and later through the written record found in the four gospels. What mighty things would have been accomplished had all the followers of Jesus made use of this power!

The words quoted at the beginning of this chapter were part of the message of Christ to twelve believers who were sent out to do the very things which I knew God had called me to do -- "Heal the sick, cleanse the lepers, raise the dead, cast out devils: freely ye have received, freely give." Matt. 10:8. With these wonderful promises of power were included warnings of persecution -- "Ye shall be brought before governors and kings for my sake." (v 18). "Brother shall deliver up brother to death, and the father the child: and the children shall rise up against their parents, and cause them to be put to death." (v 21). No deliverance from this persecution was promised to the followers of Christ, although they were to have power to do the things which He did. CHRIST HIMSELF WAS PERSECUTED. If His disciples could do the works He did, and in addition be delivered from persecution, then indeed would the disciple be above his master.

"Yea, and all that will live godly in Christ Jesus shall suffer persecution." II Tim. 3:12. Persecution is one of the universal results of manifested power.

Jesus was not persecuted while He remained in the carpenter shop at Nazareth, but the moment He started to do mighty things, He was called "Prince of devils," and attempts began to be made to destroy his life. (See Luke 4:29.) Persecutions continued for three and one-half years, until at last He was crucified, for no other reason than because He had power which the powerless religious leaders of his day feared. Peter was a "good fellow" so long as he was a mere fisherman, but when he healed the lame man, they threw him in jail. Acts 3:7; 4:3. So long as Stephen was just a "member" in the First Church at Jerusalem he got along nicely, but the moment he "did great wonders and miracles among the people" (Acts 6:8), he was called into judgment and stoned. Paul never had to flee at night for his life, because of his religion, until after he had met God in a supernatural way.

Even so, you will not meet with much opposition and persecution so long as you are just, as the world would say, a "normal Christian," but when you begin to accept God's promises for your life, and to do the UNUSUAL, persecution will come!

Personally, I met with very little opposition until I made up my mind to have all God had promised me as a minister.

This opposition may appear to come from people, but it is really directed by Satan, the commanding general of the opposing army, and using all the methods of warfare from direct frontal attack to "fifth column activities" among our own people.

Again and again, Jesus pointed out to His disciples the price of following in His steps, recommending that they count the cost, and offering them the opportunity of turning back if the price seemed too great, in proportion to the value of the blessing to be received. Our master "for the joy that was set before him endured the cross, despising the shame, and is set down at the right hand of the throne of God." Heb. 12:2.

If we suffer we shall also reign with him." II Tim. 2:12. To the disciple who seeks to share in His power and glory, it must FIRST OF ALL be pointed out that he, being not greater than his master, must follow the same path of suffering, faithfulness and consecration which his Master followed, if he is to reach the goal, if he would know the abundant life -- the powerful life -- in this world, and share in heaven's glory.

If the Son of God must suffer rejection, persecution, cruel

scourgings, and crucifixion, at the hands of those to whom He came to minister, His disciple is not above suffering in order that he may carry the gospel of deliverance to those in bondage.

If Christ Himself must reject all earthly ambitions -- even refusing the opportunity to rule the world, when that opportunity was presented aside from the principals of godliness (see Matt. 4:8-10) -- then surely His disciple, if he is to know real power, must have an eye single to the purpose of God, rejecting all offers but His, no matter how attractive they may be. His cry must be, like his Master, "Lo I come to do thy will, O God." Heb. 10:7. Like Paul, he must be able to say, "I count all things but loss for the excellency of the knowledge of Christ." Phil 3:8.

If the Son of God must spend long hours of the night, when the rest of the world was sleeping, alone on the mountain top with His Father, in order that He might be able to cast out even those demons of whom He said, "This kind goeth not out but by prayer and fasting" (Matt. 17:21), surely His disciple also must spend hours in fasting and prayer, waiting upon God -- learning to think and act in unison with God -- before he can expect to cast out such demons.

"Men ought always to pray and not to faint," Luke 18:1. Persistent, habitual prayer was one of the outstanding characteristics of the life of Christ. When Judas desired to find Jesus in order to betray Him to the priests, he knew that he would find Him in the garden of prayer. Prayer to our Lord was more important than teaching and healing, for He refused to allow Himself to be swept off His feet by the multitudes who "came together to hear, and to be healed by Him" (Luke 5:15,16), but withdrew Himself from the crowd which demanded His attention into the wilderness, and prayed. Prayer was more important to Him than the working of miracles, for miracles do not generate themselves. Prayer is the cause -- miracles the result. Prayer to Jesus was more important than rest and sleep, for we find that "in the morning rising up a great while before day, he went out and departed into a solitary place, and there prayed." Mark 1:35. And again, "He went out into a mountain to pray and he continued all night in prayer to God." Luke 6:12.

If the disciple could attain the same results which Jesus did WITHOUT PAYING THE SAME PRICE WHICH JESUS

PAID, then it would have to be confessed that the disciple
had become greater than his master. The "student" would
have learned a better, more efficient method than that
taught to him by his "teacher." In the world, this often happens. Many a musician has advanced beyond the one who
gave him his training. Many an artist has far excelled the
one who taught him to draw and paint. And many a scien-
tist has learned for himself things which his science teachers never knew. But the student of Jesus Christ CANNOT
become greater than his teacher. He cannot learn anything
which Jesus did not know. He cannot find a short cut to
power with God. If he should try it, he will only meet with
disappointment and sorrow. His life will be shipwrecked
and his ministry useless.

For the disciple (student) of Christ, "It is enough for the
disciple that he be as his master (teacher)." Matt. 10:25.

Before I could fully comprehend all which God has spoken
to me, suddenly He was speaking to me again, the words
which form the second step of the revelation which God
gave to me as I waited before Him in fasting and prayer.

# CHAPTER 3

## "THE DISCIPLE IS NOT ABOVE HIS MASTER: BUT EVERYONE THAT IS PERFECT SHALL BE AS HIS MASTER"

My spirit which had been humbled and almost crushed by the words of the first message was suddenly lifted up in a blaze of glory, as I realized that although I could never be above my Master, God had said I should be AS MY MASTER! (This I also found to be a quotation from scripture -- Luke 6:40.)

This is not a promise (as some have thought) which awaits the coming of Christ for its fulfillment. It is meant for the followers of Christ HERE AND NOW! This promise was spoken to me directly, for my own instruction and edification, but since it is a direct quotation of scripture, it does not apply to me alone, but to EVERY ONE WHO WILL BELIEVE IT! It is to YOU! You can heal the sick! You can see miracles! You can exercise the gifts of the Spirit! (I Cor. 12:8-11) YOU CAN DO THE WORKS HE DID! God has said that you could, and HE CANNOT LIE!

"God is not a man, that he should lie; neither the son of man, that he should repent: hath he said, and shall he not do it? or hath he spoken, and shall he not make it good? Num. 23:19.

"My covenant will I not break, nor alter the thing that is gone out of my lips." Ps. 89:34. Then, "Every one that is PERFECT" (that will meet the requirements, I COULD BE AS MY MASTER!

But some will say, "That is impossible, for He was God, as well as human. And we are only human."

These are unmindful of the plain statements of scripture, "Verily he took not on him the nature of angels: but he took on him the seed of Abraham. Wherefore IN ALL THINGS behooved him to be made LIKE UNTO HIS BRETHREN."

Heb. 2:16, 17.

"But made himself of no reputation, and took upon him the FORM OF A SERVANT, and was made in the LIKENESS OF MEN: And being found IN FASHION AS A MAN, he humbled himself." Phil. 2:7, 8.

"The MAN Christ Jesus." I Tim. 2:5.

One night, when Jesus and his disciples were in a small boat, there came a great storm at sea, which caused the disciples to be very fearful for their lives. Jesus rebuked the winds and the sea, and immediately there was a great calm. The men who were with him in the boat marveled, saying, "What manner of MAN is this?" Matt. 8:27.

Their question is still the cry of many today, when they observe some of His disciples, who by faith are claiming His promises, and going forth healing the sick, raising the dead, and ministering the word (as Jesus himself said they should -- Mark 16:17,18) with the supernatural confirmation of signs following. Many seem to think that these are some peculiar and different species, or manner, of men. They are not. They are simply common, ordinary men, full of the Holy Ghost, and yielded to God for his work -- men who have discovered that they can be AS THEIR MASTER, and have dedicated their lives to reaching that goal.

When the people at Lystra saw that Paul's command could bring healing to a man lame from his mother's womb, they said, "The gods are come down to us in the likeness of men." Being untaught heathen they of course did not know that men could have such power. But many Christian people seem to be just as unaware of the power which God has made available for his people. When these poor heathen people would have offered sacrifices unto Paul and Barnabas as Gods, they refused to permit this, saying. "We also are men of like passions with you, and preach unto you that ye should turn -- unto the living God." See Acts 14:8-15.

Jesus truly was God, as well as man. Yet it was not in His nature of deity that He walked upon earth and performed miracles. The often neglected question is not "What manner of God is this?" We as His disciples, need to ask as did those disciples of old, "What manner of MAN is this?"

Jesus, by His own statement, was a member of the eternal triune Godhead, composed of the Father (Jehovah), the Son

(Jesus Christ), and the Holy Ghost. He existed before the world was made, and shared in the work of creation. (John 1:1-3.) He was not only WITH God and LIKE God, HE WAS GOD! All the attributes of deity were His. With the Father, He was omnipotent, omniscient, omnipresent, and eternal. All these are His today, as He is glorified on the right hand of God in heaven. At the close of His earthly ministry of healing the sick and working miracles, when He was ready to be offered as a sacrifice for our sins, he prayed, "I have glorified thee on the earth. I have finished the work which thou gavest me to do. And now O Father, glorify thou me with thine own self WITH THE GLORY WHICH I HAD WITH THEE BEFORE THE WORLD WAS." John 17:4, 5.

The glory which was His before the world was! The glory which is His today!

But the glory which was LAID ASIDE when he took on human flesh. Coming as a helpless babe, born of a woman, circumcised like any other Jewish boy, increasing in wisdom and stature during childhood and growth (Luke 2:52), weeping, hungering, thirsting, weary, sleeping and waking -- partaking in every weakness and limitation of human flesh and blood. (Forasmuch then as the children are partakers of flesh and blood, he also HIMSELF LIKEWISE TOOK PART OF THE SAME. Heb. 2:14.) He was "IN ALL POINTS tempted like as we are, yet without sin." Heb. 4:15.

He was "in the beginning with God. All things were made by Him; and without him was not anything made that was made." John 1:2, 3. Yet for all this, Jesus USED NO POWER when He was here on earth in the flesh WHICH IS NOT AVAILABLE TODAY to every believer! Such a statement would be blasphemy HAD NOT JESUS HIMSELF made it plain, again and again, that this was His plan.

"Everyone that is perfect SHALL BE AS HIS MASTER." Luke 6:40.

"As thou hast send me into the world, EVEN SO have I also sent them into the world." John 17:18.

"The works that I do SHALL HE DO ALSO." John 14:12.

Although He was Omnipotent God, yet in His earthly life and ministry He declared "The son can do nothing of himself." "I can of mine own self do nothing." John 5:19,30. "The words that I speak unto you I speak NOT OF MYSELF: But the Father that dwelleth in me, he doeth the works."

John 14:10.

The answer to the disciples' question, "What manner of MAN is this?" is found not in the powers of deity which He used before He "was made flesh and dwelt among us," nor in the power which is His today in the heavenlies today. The answer can be found only in His earthly (human) life. He lived that life AS AN EXAMPLE to those whom He left in the world to finish the work which he had started while He was here. "Leaving us an EXAMPLE, that YE should follow his steps." I Pet. 2:21. He was our teacher (master) and we, His disciples (every one that is perfect), SHALL BE AS our master! Had He used power which was not available to us, it would be impossible for us to follow His example. But He left to us the promise that we would receive THE SAME POWER and from the SAME SOURCE, that was His!

"Behold I send the promise of my Father upon you: but tarry ye in the city of Jerusalem, until ye be endued with POWER FROM ON HIGH." Luke 24:49.

"Ye shall receive POWER after that the Holy Ghost is come upon you." Acts 1:8.

These signs shall follow them that believe: IN MY NAME they shall cast out devils; they shall speak with new tongues -- they shall lay hands on the sick and they shall recover." Mark 16:17, 18.

"Behold, I give unto you POWER -- over all the power of the enemy." Luke 10:19.

"He that believeth on me, THE WORKS THAT I DO SHALL HE DO ALSO." John 14:12. "Though he was rich (in heavenly glory and divine power) yet for your sakes he became poor, THAT YE THROUGH HIS POVERTY MIGHT BE RICH." II Cor. 8:9 He folded it all away as a garment, and laid aside His great wealth of power, and came into the world as a babe, in the form of a servant, of no reputation, lived among men as one of them. (Phil. 2:7.) Tradition has invented miracles in his childhood, but the Word of God plainly declares that "This BEGINNING of miracles did Jesus in Cana of Galilee," (where He turned water into wine). John 2:11. He DID NO MIRACLE nor manifested any superhuman power, BEFORE THE HOLY SPIRIT DESCENDED UPON HIM! (Matt. 3:16, 17; John 1:33.) It was when "God anointed Jesus of Nazareth with the HOLY GHOST AND WITH POWER" that he "went about doing good, and healing all that were oppressed of the devil; FOR GOD WAS WITH HIM." Acts 10:38. This is the secret of His success AS A MAN.

What manner of man?

A man ANOINTED WITH THE HOLY GHOST AND WITH POWER. And God was WITH HIM!

Yet -- don't forget this -- a man who was EVERY INCH A MAN! A man who faced -- and conquered -- EVERY TEMP-TATION known to humanity! A man who (though as God, He had been omnipresent) could only be in one place at a time. Although as God He had neither slumbered nor slept (Ps. 121:4), as man, He suffered weariness (John 4:6) and required sleep (Matt. 8:24). He must go from place to place upon hot, weary, dusty feet -- His rate of travel limited to the speed of walking, His feet which had trod the immacu-late golden streets of heaven soiled and bruised by the dust and stones of the unpaved and filthy Oriental streets and paths of Palestine. How He welcomed the cleansing cool-ness of the customary foot bath before meals -- when some unselfish person thought to minister to Him in this way! He suffered hunger and thirst, loneliness, weariness, and pain. He of whom it had been said, "Every beast of the forest is mine, and the cattle upon a thousand hills. The world is mine and the fullness thereof" (Ps. 50:10, 12), claimed no part of it for Himself AS A MAN, but became even more poor than the foxes and birds, for He had not so much as a place to lay His head. (Luke 9:58).

All this He did WILLINGLY for us, that we might share the riches of His glory.

When Satan tempted Him in the wilderness (Matt. 4:3, 4), the first temptation was that He should act in the creative power of the ETERNAL SON OF GOD, in order that His hu-man hunger might be satisfied. Had He done this, He would have failed in being "in all points like unto his brethren." It was important to the plan of Satan that this point should, if possible, be spoiled. But Jesus did not fall into this temp-tation. In His reply is no assumption of deity. He answered firmly AS A MAN! "MAN shall not live by bread alone, but by every word that proceedeth out of the mouth of God."

He loved to refer to Himself as the "SON OF MAN."

Since it is so apparent by the scripture that Jesus took upon Himself our own nature and limitations, in order that He might be made a proper example for us, it behooves us to study that example carefully, considering the question, "What manner of persons OUGHT YE TO BE in all holy conversation and godliness." II Pet. 3:11.

He was a man of power. He spoke as one having authority (Mark 1:22). The people were astonished at this, for the religious leaders of their day knew nothing of this power, but taught traditions and theories and theological explanations. Jesus cut across all the lines drawn by their fine points of doctrine, and DROVE OUT BY HIS WORDS OF AUTHORITY demons, sickness and infirmity. When he spoke THINGS HAPPENED! He spoke as one having authority BECAUSE HE HAD AUTHORITY! The traditional religious leaders did not speak as He spoke because they had never been given authority over the power of the enemy. How many "religious" leaders today speak as the scribes and Pharisees! Those who are LIKE their master speak with authority -- the authority which was Christ's while He was here to use it, because He had received it from the Father (John 5:27). He came in the Father's name (John 5:43), and His legal works of His Father. ("I must work the works of him that sent me." John 9:4.) While He was on earth He chose disciples (first twelve, Luke 9:1, then seventy others, Luke 10:1, 19) which He appointed as "deputies," giving them the same power of attorney which He used. ("Lord, even the devils are subject unto us THROUGH THY NAME." Luke 10:17.) Thus were they trained under His direct supervision to be ready to carry forward "all that Jesus BEGAN both to do and to teach" (Acts 1:1), when the time should come for Him to return to the Father.

Having now returned to the Father, and being on the right hand of God exalted, He has not planned that the work which He began through such suffering and sacrifice should cease to be carried forward. Before He went away, He left command and authority for the continuation of His work. Those who believe on Him are made His agents, and are commanded to do IN HIS NAME (by His authority, as by the power of attorney) all the things which He Himself would do if He were present in the body! "IN MY NAME shall they cast out devils; they shall speak with new tongues; they shall take up serpents (not as tempting God, but should it so happen by accident, as it did to Paul, Acts 28:3-5) and if they drink any deadly thing it shall not hurt them; they shall lay hands on the sick, and they shall recover." Mark 16:17,18. "And whatsoever ye shall ask IN MY NAME, that will I do, that the Father may be glorified in the Son." John 14:13.

The gifts which He placed in the church, for the perfecting of the saints, for the work of the ministry, for the edifying (up-building) of the body of Christ (His church), Eph. 4:8-12, cover all the great and mighty things which Jesus did when He was here in the flesh (see I Cor. 12:7-11).

Never once did He teach, either by inference or by direct statement, that this power would be gone from the world when He went away. Rather, in his last commission to those He left behind, He declared, "All power is given unto me in heaven and in earth. GO YE THEREFORE (because this power is HIS, and through Him OURS, Luke 24:49, Acts 1:8) and teach ALL NATIONS -- teaching them to OBSERVE (obey -- Webster's definition) ALL THINGS (Heal the sick, cleanse the lepers, raise the dead, cast out devils, freely ye have received, freely give. Matt. 10:8.) whatsoever I have commanded you: and lo, I am with you always, even unto the end of the world. Amen." Matt. 28:18-20.

These disciples, anointed with the Holy Ghost (Acts 2:4), "went forth and preached everywhere, the Lord was working WITH THEM, and confirming the word with SIGNS FOLLOWING." Mark 16:20.

So long as men are anointed with the Holy Ghost, and God is with them, as it was with Jesus (Acts 10:38) and the early disciples (Mark 16:20) and as Jesus said it should be "even unto the end of the world" (Matt. 28:20), the works Jesus did will continue to be done!

The disciple should not be above his master, but he SHALL BE AS HIS MASTER!

But if we are to be like Him in POWER, we must also be like Him in holiness, in consecration, in meekness, in compassion. We must be like Him in prayer and in fellowship with the Father. We must be like Him in faith. We must be like Him in fasting and self-denial. If it were possible for the servant to be like Him in power without paying the price He paid, then the servant would be above his Lord.

There is a price to be paid for all that God offers to mankind. In a sense, it is all free, but there is a price of obedience and preparedness. Even our free salvation is ours only when we have heeded the admonition of God to repent and believe upon the Lord Jesus Christ. The "gift of the Holy Ghost" is ours only when we obey Him. Acts 5:32. Power with God LIKE JESUS HAD is for those -- ALL THOSE -- who meet the condition, "every one that is PERFECT shall be as his master." Luke 6:40.

# CHAPTER 4

## "BE YE THEREFORE PERFECT, EVEN AS YOUR FATHER IN HEAVEN IS PERFECT"

These words seemed even more startling than the ones which God had already spoken. Surely this was too much! Could any mortal ever hope to be perfect? Yet surely God would not ask me to do something which He knew I could not do! And without doubt, this was the voice of God. I had asked bread of my heavenly Father, and I knew that He would not give me a stone. How thrilling to my soul when I learned that this, too, was a quotation from scripture! I found it in

Matt. 5:48. It was Christ's own command, not only to me but to all who would be the "children of your Father which is in heaven" (verse 45). Perfection is the GOAL set by Christ for every Christian. Not every Christian has reached that goal. No Christian has a right to boast that he has attained it. Even the great Apostle Paul declared, "Not as though I had already attained, either were already perfect, but I follow after" (Phil 3:12). No Christian worthy of the name will be satisfied to be less than perfect. No Christian should make excuse for his own imperfections, but should recognize them as failure to keep the command of Christ, and strive earnestly to overcome them. PERFECTION IS THE GOAL!

For the benefit of those who may have been taught that no person except Christ was ever perfect, let us note that GOD HIMSELF ascribes perfection to a number of men. They did not claim perfection for themselves, but God declared that they were perfect.

First of all, Job, the hero of the oldest written book of the Bible was a perfect man. His friends didn't think he was perfect; they accused him of hypocrisy (see Job 8:6,13.) Satan did not think he was perfect; he accused him of serving

God only because of the material blessings which God had given him. Job himself was willing to admit that he was imperfect, for he declared, "I abhor myself, and repent in dust and ashes," Job 42:6. But when Satan accused him before the Lord, God himself declared, "Hast thou considered my servant Job, that there is none like him in the earth, a PERFECT AND AN UPRIGHT MAN?" Job 1:8. And then for the benefit of all who might read this scripture, God added his definition of human perfection -- "one that feareth God and escheweth (shunneth, avoideth) evil."

Many object to the teaching of possible perfection on the grounds that they have never seen a perfect man. In Job's day, God declared that there was only one. Again, in Noah's day there was only one. Yet God declares that Noah was PERFECT! "Noah was a just man and PERFECT in his generations, and Noah walked with God." Gen. 6:9.

Some declare that if one should become perfect, he would immediately be translated, as was Enoch, carelessly disregarding the fact that the scripture declares that Enoch 'walked with God" for at least three hundred years before he "was not", Gen 5:22, and that "BEFORE his translation he had this testimony, that he pleased God." Heb. 11:5.

All these Old Testament saints were perfect, before even the law was given. No divinity, nor superhuman perfection is attributed to any one of them. They were MEN, subject to like passions as we are, but they knew and feared God, kept his commands, and carefully avoided the overflowing evils of the idolatrous people among whom they lived, in some of the most outstandingly evil ages in history.

Was perfection possible under the law?

Moses, speaking God's message to the entire congregation of Israel, declared "Thou shalt be PERFECT with the Lord thy God." Deut. 18:13.

Man is sometimes more critical than God. When Miriam and Aaron complained against Moses, God took his part, speaking to them out of the pillar of cloud and saying, "My servant Moses -- is FAITHFUL in all mine house!" Numbers 12:7. While this does not use the word "perfect", surely it meets the definition given in Job 1:8.

David was not persuaded that perfection was impossible, for he declared, in one of his inspired Psalms, "I will behave myself wisely IN A PERFECT WAY. I will walk within my house with a PERFECT HEART." Ps. 101:2.

All these, and no doubt many others (such as Daniel, Joseph, Abraham, Elijah, and Elisha, etc.) lived lives of holiness (perfection) in the days before many of our advantages were given. It was to his New Testament church that God gave the complete scriptures. "ALL scripture is given by inspiration of God, and is profitable -- that the man of God may be PERFECT, thoroughly furnished unto all good works. II Tim. 3:16, 17.

It was not until our own dispensation that Christ was preached, "Whom we preach, warning every man, and teaching every man in all wisdom; that we may present every man PERFECT in Christ Jesus." Col. 2:28.

It was to his New Testament Church that Christ gave apostles, prophets, evangelists, pastors and teachers "FOR THE PERFECTING OF THE SAINTS, for the work of the ministry, for the EDIFYING OF THE BODY OF CHRIST." Eph. 4:11, 12.

Unto them, the glorious outpouring of the Holy Spirit, our constantly abiding Comforter, teacher and guide, (John 14:26) had not been given. But to us he is given -- to everyone who will obey God (Acts 5:32).

How much easier it should be for us, with all these advantages, to be perfect than for those who lived before these things were given!

God says to us, "Ye are the temple of the living God: as God hath said, I will dwell in them and walk in them . . . . Wherefore come ye out from among them, and be ye separate, saith the Lord, and touch not the unclean thing, and I will receive you, and will be a Father unto you and ye shall be my sons and daughters, saith the Lord Almighty. Having therefore these promises, dearly beloved, let us cleanse ourselves from ALL filthiness of the flesh and spirit, PERFECTING HOLINESS in the fear of God." II Cor. 6:16-7:1.

These promises are ours! We CAN cleanse ourselves from ALL FILTHINESS! We can PERFECT HOLINESS in the fear of God! Like Job, we can fear God and shun evil, and be perfect in the sight of God.

This is not a "new thing". The doctrine of entire sanctification has been taught by many outstanding servants of Christ throughout the church age, and is accepted as sound doctrine by a number of major denominations. Since this is only a small book, space prevents quoting from the statements of fundamental truths of many groups. I will quote here from only one, that found in the Constitution of the General Council of the Assemblies of God. (Minutes and Constitution, with Bylaws, Revised (1949 edition), Page 38, Section 9.) Entire Sanctification (br)

The Scriptures teach a life of holiness without which no man shall see the Lord. By the power of the Holy Ghost we are able to obey the command, "Be ye holy, for I am Holy." Entire sanctification is the will of God for all believers, and should be earnestly pursued by walking in obedience to God's Word. Heb. 12:14; I Peter 1:15, 16; I Thess. 5:23, 24; I John 2:6."

Call it what you will -- perfection, holiness, entire sanctification -- it is not only possible, it is not only our privilege, it is God's COMMAND.

"Be ye holy in ALL MANNER OF CONVERSATION." I Peter 1:15. "Be ye therefore perfect." Matt. 5:48.

You say, "I know a lot of Christians, even preachers, who say you can't be perfect, and there is no use to try."

We know them, too. They are not healing the sick nor casting out demons! Sin is the devil's bridgehead in your life. Let him hold the bridgehead, if you will. But it will rob you of power!

Jesus did not allow the devil to maintain a bridgehead in his life, for he declared just before he was crucified, "The prince of this world (Satancometh, and hath NOTHING in me." John 14:30. He had power to accomplish the work he came into the world to do because Satan had NOTHING -- not even one little bridgehead of pet sin or self-indulgence -- in Him.

We, his followers, are admonished to keep the coasts of our lives free of "bridgeheads" too. "Neither give PLACE to the devil." Eph. 4:27. It is his business to make you think that you can't expect to keep your life entirely free of his hideouts and landing strips. If he can get you to leave him a place to work from, he can sabotage every effort you make for God, and rob you of the power you have longed for. The work God has given you to do will go undone. The sick will not be healed, the captives not set free. Should you attempt to cast out demons, they will laugh in your face, saying, "You let us remain in your own life, and then would cast us out of others!" Demons know the power of Christ, and they know and fear the power of a Christ filled Christian. But they have no fear of one who is not holy.

Seven sons of one Sceva, a Jew and chief of the priests, decided that they could say the same words which Paul used, adjuring the demons in Jesus name to come out of those who were possessed, without being careful to have the background of holiness and consecration which Paul had. (See Acts 19:13-15). The evil spirit answered and said, "Jesus I know, and Paul I know; but WHO ARE YE?! Then the man in whom the evil spirit was, leaped on them, and overcame them, so that they fled naked and wounded. They didn't think holiness was necessary, but they found to their sorrow that it CAN NOT BE OVERLOOKED, if one is to exercise the miracle working power of God! The reaction is not so immediate and violent in every case, for these "vagabond Jews" had tried it before, and only once did this happen. But never once did they succeed in casting out a demon. Demons flee only before the power of Christ, or of a Christ-filled life. There is no way to have power with God without holiness -- for Jesus himself said, "Every one that is PERFECT shall be AS HIS MASTER." Luke 6:40.

There is much that could be said about perfection. An entire book could easily be written in defense of the possibility of obeying the command of God, "Be ye holy, for I am holy." I Peter 1:16. However, enough has been said to open the eyes of the person who is hungry for truth, and eager to have the power which Jesus promised to his followers, THE MIRACLE WORKING POWER OF GOD.

But it will take more than knowing that holiness is possible. You want to know how you can attain it.

Not every Christian has reached the goal. Not every follower of Christ has the power which he promised. The twelve chosen disciples, even after having healed many that were sick and cast out many demons in Jesus' name, met a demon one day who refused to go at their command. Matt. 17:15. When Jesus had cast out the demon, the disciples asked him why they could not do it. He gave as the reason their UNBELIEF, and lack of fasting and prayer. These twelve chosen men were at times found to lack in the manifestation of the fruits of the Spirit, and to show evidence of such works of the flesh as pride (Mark 10:37),

jealousy (Mark 10:41), anger (Matt. 26:51). They slept when
they should have prayed (Matt. 26:40), and deserted him in
times of trial (vs. 56). They failed to discern the plan of God,
and rebuked Jesus because he told them that he would be
killed, so that Jesus said to one of them, "Get thee behind
me, Satan: -- Thou savourest not the things that be of God,
but those that be of men." Matt. 16:23. These men had not
reached perfection, but they earnestly desired to be perfect,
and worked diligently to attain the promises of God, and
God honored them, and was not ashamed to be called their
God.

Do not be discouraged because you have not attained
unto perfection. There is an ultimate perfection which will
only be reached when we see Jesus face to face at his coming. There is a growth in grace, growing toward perfection,
which must continue so long as we remain in the flesh. Our
perfection may be likened to the fruit on a tree. From the
time the bud appears, the apple on the inside, though very
tiny, can be perfect. It has not taken on the size, color, nor
flavor which it will eventually have, but nevertheless in its
present state it is perfect. As it is nourished, and fed, and
protected from frost and disease -- as the sun and the rain
touch it, and the heat and the cold, it grows into a perfect
little green apple, and finally the large, beautiful, rich, full-
ripe fruit.

It was this "unripe fruit" perfection which Paul referred
to in Phil. 3:15 -- "Let US (including himself) therefore, as
many as be PERFECT be thus minded." Three verses before,
he had said, "Not as though I had already attained, either
were ALREADY PERFECT." (v. 12.) Here he was speaking of
the ultimate perfection of the full ripe fruit, the perfection
which will only be complete with the resurrection of the
dead. Paul was not unmindful of the perfection which had
already been attained, but with the true Christian spirit,
he was not satisfied to remain in that state, but, though
he didn't claim to be perfect, declared, "I follow after." "This
one thing I do, forgetting those things which are behind,
and reaching forward to those things which are before, I
PRESS TOWARD THE MARK." (v. 12, 13, 14.)

There is no stopping place short of ultimate perfection.
Although the immature Christian may be perfect in God's
sight, HE WILL CEASE TO BE PERFECT WHEN HE IS

WILLING TO STOP GROWING! When the little green apple stops growing, it will soon wither and fall from the tree. Perfection must be attained, and constantly striven for.

Growth must be maintained through FOOD "Desire the sincere milk of the word (the Bible) that ye may grow thereby." I Peter 2:2. A good appetite for the word of God is very necessary if we are to "grow in grace and in the knowledge of our Lord and Savior." 2 Pet. 2:2. A real love for the Word of God is a part of our perfection NOW, and means much toward our ultimate perfection when Jesus comes. "All scripture is given by inspiration of God and is profitable for doctrine, for reproof, for correction, for instruction in righteousness: that the man of God MAY BE PERFECT." 2 Tim. 3:16, 17.

Many have plenty of time to read comic strips, magazine, novels -- everything else but the Word of God. But they are just too busy to study their Bibles! No wonder they do not grow! No wonder they have no power to heal the sick and cast out demons. No wonder they are not perfect, and do not expect to be. They are not feeding their souls the right food. "Grow in grace and in the KNOWLEDGE of our Lord and Savior." 2 Pet. 2:3. This knowledge comes through study of God's word. Read it a great deal. And read it as God's revelation to you. Believe it as you read it. It is the word of Him who cannot lie. He means EXACTLY WHAT HE SAYS!

Ample protection is provided for those who abide in Christ. Whatever our temptations may be, we need not sin for "God is faithful, who will not suffer you to be tempted above that ye are able, but with temptation also make a way of escape that ye may be able to bear it." I Cor. 10:13.

"He that hath begun a good work in you will perform it until the day of Jesus Christ." Phil 1:6. The Lord is faithful, who shall establish you and KEEP YOU FROM EVIL." 2 Thes. 3:3.

"Now unto him that is able to keep you from falling and to present you FAULTLESS before the presence of his glory." Jude 24.

Hallelujah! It is possible to be kept by God, and to live on a higher plane than sin.

We are not ignorant of the devices of Satan. He can quote scripture, too. How quickly he comes to comfort the imperfect Christian, by quoting the last half of Matt. 26:41 -- "The spirit indeed is willing, but the flesh is weak." This portion should never be quoted without the first part of the verse -- "Watch and pray, that ye ENTER NOT INTO TEMPTATION!" Thus may we overcome the weakness of the flesh.

Walk in the Spirit, and ye shall not fulfill the lust of the flesh." Gal. 5:16. (You may be sure Satan will not add this passage to his quotation.) "Now the works of the flesh are manifest -- of the which I tell you -- that they which do such things SHALL NOT INHERIT THE KINGDOM OF GOD." Gal. 5:19-21.

"For to be CARNALLY (fleshly) MINDED is death." Rom. 8:6.

Hide behind the weakness of the flesh if you like, but do not overlook what God says will be the result! Do not accept Satan's suggestion, even when he quotes scripture. "RESIST THE DEVIL AND HE WILL FLEE FROM YOU!" James 4:7.

You can be perfect! God says you can. Only Satan says you cannot.

God has provided food for you in his word, protection for you through his spirit, and a mighty agency for your perfecting in his Church. In order that the church might serve to this end, "He gave some, apostles; and some, prophets: and some, evangelists; and some, pastors and teachers; for the PERFECTING of the saints --." Eph. 4:11, 12.

Do not think that you shall attain the perfection which God desires for you if you fail to heed his warning, "Not forsaking the assembling of yourselves together, as the manner of some is." Heb. 10:25. Find a good church home, where God's word is taught and BELIEVED, where the power of God is present and welcome, where God is confirming his word with signs following, and where God's people "Speak the things which become SOUND DOCTRINE." Titus 2:1. Then make it a practice to be present whenever God and his people meet. Only thus can you be perfected by the ministry gifts which God has placed in the church. Every service in your Spirit filled church is planned of God to contribute something to your perfection.

Patience also has a part. "Let patience have her perfect work that ye may be PERFECT AND ENTIRE wanting nothing." Jas. 1:4.

The tongue also plays an important part, for "If any man offend not in word, the same is a

PERFECT man and able also to bridle the whole body." James 3:2.

"And above all these things put on charity, which is the bond of perfectness." Col. 3:14. Christ is sufficiently interested in pointing out the way, that if you desire to find the way of perfectness, he will place his finger on your pet sins, and show you what is keeping you from the goal. A young man once fell at the feet of Jesus and asked the question, "What must I do?" Although this young man was inquiring the way of salvation, Jesus pointed out to him the way to perfection. "If thou wilt be PERFECT, go ----." Matt. 19:21. He laid his finger upon the young man's pet sin. Like so many others the young man felt that this was too much. Yet it would have been a small price to pay for perfection here, and eternal life in the world to come. Jesus is just the same today. When you come inquiring how you can be perfect, he will not send you away without an answer.

Perfection and more perfection is always the Christian goal. "I press toward the mark for the prize of the high calling of God in Christ Jesus. Let us therefore, AS MANY AS BE PERFECT, be thus minded: and if in anything ye be otherwise minded, GOD SHALL REVEAL EVEN THIS UNTO YOU." Phil. 3:14, 15.

As you read this book, Satan will probably whisper to you many times, as Pharaoh said unto Moses (Ex. 8:25) "Sacrifice in the land." In other words, it isn't necessary to go so far, to separate yourself from the things of the world in order to have power with God. If you insist, he will say, "All right then, only don't go too far." He infers there is danger in going too far.

You can't go too far with God. You may go too far in sin. You may go too far in self-righteousness. But if you are walking with Jesus, in the Spirit, you need not fear going too far. No believer has gone as far as God wants him to go until the signs follow his ministry. We have not gone as far as we should go until we can lay hands on the sick and see them recover! No church has gone as far as the Lord meant it should go until all nine gifts of the spirit are in operation in its services. DON'T LET PHARAOH (SATAN) KEEP YOU BACK! Go on! Go all the way. God's grace is sufficient for you. Don't let anything keep you from appropriating the promises of God in your own life, whether you be lay member or minister.

# CHAPTER 5

## CHRIST OUR EXAMPLE

"For even hereunto were ye called; because Christ also suffered for us, LEAVING US AN EXAMPLE, that ye should FOLLOW HIS STEPS; who did no sin, neither was guile found in his mouth; who when he was reviled, reviled not again; when he suffered, he threatened not; but committed himself to him that judgeth righteously." I Peter 2:21-23.

This scripture makes it very plain to any honest hearted child of God that Christ is OUR EXAMPLE in WORD and in DEED! We can, then, WALK AS CHRIST WALKED, and we can TALK AS HE TALKED. This is not a condition of one's feet or lips, but of the HEART! "For from within, out of the heart of man, proceed evil thoughts, adulteries, fornications, murders, thefts, covetousness, wickedness, deceit, lasciviousness, an evil eye, blasphemy, pride, foolishness: all these evil things come from within, and defile a man." Mark 7:21-23.

For as he thinketh in his heart, so is he." Prov. 23:7.

Before one can walk as Christ walked, and talk as he talked, he must first begin to THINK AS CHRIST THOUGHT! This is possible only as we "Bring into captivity every thought to the obedience of Christ." II Cor. 10:5. This doesn't just happen. It is an act of determined consecration, requiring purpose and continual application, for the mind loves to wander. It also requires a willing exchange, giving up the former ways of thinking, and accepting as our own the MIND OF CHRIST. "LET this mind be in you which was also in Christ Jesus." Phil. 2:5.

God draws the line on some thinking. It is possible to lead a victorious thought life. Not that Satan can no longer come with evil suggestions. Nowhere in God's word has He declared that man would not be tempted. Even Christ was tempted. But one can refuse to allow his thought to dwell upon evil things. A sane mind is a controlled mind. Evil thoughts can be driven out, by filling the mind with right thoughts. We are instructed as to what these thoughts are. "Finally, brethren, whatsoever things are true, whatsoever things are honest, whatsoever things are just, whatsoever things are pure, whatsoever things are lovely, whatsoever things are of good report; if there be any virtue, and if there be any praise, THINK ON THESE THINGS." Phil. 4:8.

Jesus thought right thoughts. That was the reason that he could walk and talk right, and be a right example for us to follow.

"Christ suffered for us, leaving us an example, that we should follow his steps, WHO DID NO SIN." I Pet. 2:21, 22. Christ did not live in habitual sin. He did not make excuses for sin. He resisted the devil, and temptation, although he was "Tempted in all points like as we are, yet without sin." Heb. 4:15. He is our example. And He stands ready to help us to walk as He walked -- in his steps! "Whosoever abideth in him sinneth not." I John 3:6.

This is contrary to much of the religious teaching today. I am aware of this. I am also aware that multitudes of religious people today, even many who believe in divine healing, find themselves powerless when faced with those who need deliverance from sickness, or demon possession. If you really want power with God, surely this matter is worthy of serious, prayerful thought, regardless of former opinions or religious teaching. There is a reason why some have power and some do not. And it is not because God is a respecter of persons. Power is a direct result of faith, and faith comes by obedience.

"Beloved, if our heart condemn us not, then have we confidence (faith) toward God, and whatsoever we ask, we receive of him, because we keep his commandments, and do those things that are pleasing in his sight." I John 3:21, 22.

Hope is available to people without holiness, BUT FAITH IS NOT!

If faith were available to people without holiness, then people who can never see God could have power to ask and receive ANYTHING THEY DESIRE from God, for God's unqualified promise to those who have faith is, "Whatsoever ye shall ask in prayer, BELIEVING YE SHALL RECEIVE." Matt. 21:22. And God has also said, "Follow peace . . . and holiness, WITHOUT WHICH NO MAN SHALL SEE THE LORD." Heb. 12:14.

Although many religious teachers declare that everyone sins all the time; that it is impossible to live above sin; that as long as one is in this world he must partake of a certain number of sins of this life; that one must sin every day, and repent every night;--God's word still calmly, simply states the command of God, "BE YE HOLY, FOR I AM HOLY." I Peter 1:16.

Paul writing to the Corinthians, declared, "Awake to righteousness and SIN NOT, for some have not the knowledge of God. I speak this to your shame." I Cor. 15:34.

People who are finding excuse for their habitual sin, according to this verse, have not the knowledge of God. This is a SHAME! It is evidence that many professed Christians are spiritually ASLEEP! They are not led by the spirit of God nor by the word of God, for the work of the spirit is to reprove the world of sin and of righteousness, (John 16:8), and the word hidden in the heart will prevent sinning against God. (Ps. 119:11.)

You can't have power when you are asleep. WAKE UP! Quit making excuses for sin. Walk in the steps of him who DID NO SIN!

"Neither was guile found in his mouth." I Peter 2:22.

Jesus healed by HIS WORD. (See Matt. 8:16.) "His word was with power." Luke 4:32. The follower of Christ is assured that his words may also be words of power. (Matt. 21:21.) But if our words are to be words of power, we must talk as he talked. Guile (cunning craftiness, deceit) must not be found in our mouths.

Jesus WALKED IN THE SPIRIT. We who are his followers are also exhorted to walk in the spirit. (Gal. 5:16.) In verses 19 to 21 are listed the works of the flesh, which are not present in the lives of those who walk in the Spirit. There are some who harbor some of these works of the flesh in their lives, making very little if any effort to overcome, who yet feel that God should honor their word and their prayer, and give them miracle working power. Yet verse 21 tells us that they which do such things shall not only fail to have power, but "SHALL NOT INHERIT THE KINGDOM OF GOD." How could one who is not even fit for the kingdom of God expect to have power to work the works of Christ?

By studying this list of "works of the flesh" with a dictionary, you will find that God has listed uncleanness, lustfulness, immoderate desire, covetousness, hatred, discord, quarreling, contention, jealousy, violent anger, rage, riotous feasting, "and such like".

Those who do such things are NOT walking in his steps who DID NO SIN, NEITHER WAS GUILE FOUND IN HIS MOUTH.

Paul exhorts us to "Put off the old man (or, works of the flesh -- see context) with his deeds," and "put on the NEW MAN, which is renewed in knowledge after the image of him that created him." Col. 3:9-10.

Listed below are some of the characteristics of the person who is carnal, and is not walking in the spirit. This list, though incomplete, may open up new channels of thought for many.

PRIDE; important, independent spirit, stiffness, or precisiveness.

LOVE OF PRAISE; love to be noticed; love of supremacy; drawing attention to one's self, as in conversation.

ARGUING; talkative spirit; stubborn, unteachable spirit; self-will; unyielding; headstrong disposition; driving, commanding spirit; criticizing spirit; peevishness; fretfulness; love to be coaxed and humored.

Speaking of faults and failures of others rather than of virtues of those more talented and appreciated than yourself.

Lustful stirrings, unholy actions, undue affection and familiarity toward the opposite sex. Wandering eyes.

Dishonest, deceitful disposition; evading or covering the truth; leaving a better impression of yourself than is true; exaggeration, or straining the truth. Selfishness; love for money; love for ease; laziness.

Formality; spiritual deadness; lack of concern for souls; dryness and indifference. LACK OF POWER WITH GOD!

Get on your knees before God, and let him talk to you about these things, and give you a list of your own. You may find that there will be many other things which are now present in your life, which God will show you MUST BE CHANGED.

A good check up on the things which we do, say, and think is to ask yourself the question, "Would Jesus do this?" If He would you are following his steps. If He would not, you are missing the mark. You cannot have power with God. You may even fail to reach heaven.

Such a life of holiness is not impossible. God has commanded it, and "He that hath begun a good work in you will perform it --" Phil. 1:6.

"Is anything too hard for the Lord?" Gen. 18:14. God said to Paul, "My grace is sufficient for thee". His grace is sufficient for you as well.

IF YOU REALLY WANT HOLINESS it is not beyond your reach.

And without it you will never share in GOD'S MIRACLE WORKING POWER!

# CHAPTER 6

## SELF DENIAL

"If any man will come after me, let him DENY HIMSELF, and take up his cross daily, and follow me." Luke 9:23. The path that Jesus walked is a way of self-denial.

You are reading this book because you desire to "come after him." Then DENY YOURSELF! Someone once said, "No man spoke as this man! Few have learned to deny self.

While we read in the scripture of Jesus, "Rising up A GREAT WHILE BEFORE DAY, he went out, and departed into a solitary place and there prayed". (Mark 1:35) How many of those who would do the works he did, find little or no time for prayer. How few of them can bear solitude. Yes, often they pray beautifully in a crowd, or when others may be listening. But the lonely hours of the night spent in solitary prayer bring no glory to SELF. Self would rather turn a little, to find a more comfortable spot on his comfortable bed, and drift softly back to sleep. Self says, "I must have my rest." Self will raise his hand smilingly, when asked who will pray an hour during the night or early morning. Self will rejoice that he has been seen taking this sacrificial hour, and how well his neighbors will think of him. But self will turn off the alarm when it sounds, and go back to sleep. Self says, "It does no good to pray anyway, when you don't feel like it." Jesus said, "Let him DENY HIMSELF." This is sacrifice -- real sacrifice to God. And God honors sacrifice.

In one of my early meetings, in southern Missouri, good crowds had been attending for a week, but not one soul had responded to the altar call. My wife and I decided that this MUST be changed, and agreed between ourselves that we would pray all night for souls to be saved in that meeting. Already we were weary in body, for the hour was late, and the service had been a hard one. Soon weariness began to creep down upon us, and even to stay awake seemed almost impossible. Again and again one must waken the other. There was no shouting, no excitement -- nothing to keep us awake but the knowledge that in this little community which God had given to us as our responsibility, souls were lost, and we must see them saved. And we had promised God to pray it through. As the sun crept over the eastern horizon, we knew that we had kept our vow, and that something was going to happen that night. We could hardly wait for the time of the service. And that night, victory came. One after another responded to the call, until nineteen souls had found salvation, and were shouting the praises of God in a little country schoolhouse, under the ministry of a preacher who had only been preaching three weeks. As we went home rejoicing from that service, we knew that God had taught us a lesson -- it pays to DENY SELF the rest he may think is rightly his. It pays to pray it through, whether self is stimulated by any good feelings, or urge to pray, or not.

SELF says, "Pray if you feel like it." SELF DENIAL says, "PRAY ANYWAY."

There are times when prayer is a delight -- when it is a time of refreshing to the weary soul. But there are times when prayer is meeting the enemy face to face upon the battleground of the world, to drag by force from his grasp the things which by God's promise are rightly ours, but which Satan will keep us from having, if he can possibly do so. There are times when we must wrestle in prayer, as did Jacob, when he cried, "I will not let thee go, except thou bless me." Gen. 32:26. There are times when the answer is slow in coming, and we must hold on patiently as did Daniel, for three full weeks (Dan. 10:2). There are times when this wrestling may leave the body weary, and the nerves overwrought, as in the case of Elijah when he had prayed down the fire and the rain (See I Kings 18, and 19:4). At times like that, prayer requires self-denial. But it pays. Only the person who BELIEVES in the power of prayer will deny himself the rest which his body demands, in order to pray. And God's promise is "Whatsoever ye shall ask in prayer, BELIEVING, ye shall receive." Matt. 21:22.

Real prayer -- determined, prevailing prayer -- is the greatest outlet of power on earth. The early church prayed ten days and then -- the miracle of Pentecost.

Moses spent forty days in the mountain talking with God, and his face shone so that he wore a veil.

Muller prayed, and secured one million dollars, making possible the care of 2,000 orphans.

Jesus went upon the mountain to pray, and returned to cast out demons which go forth only by prayer and fasting. (Mark 9:29.) He did not say to the sorrowing father, "This kind goeth not out but by prayer and fasting. Wait while I go away to fast and pray." He had already fasted and prayed! Self-denial, fasting and prayer, was a part of his daily life. It was his habit of life. He prayed first, and when the need arose, he was already "prayed through", and ready to meet the need.

How many think they are denying self, when their self-denial is only for selfish ends, to make their voice to be heard on high. (See Isa. 58:3-7.)

Fasting is an important part of self-denial. The desire for food -- the richest, the tastiest, and the best -- is one of the strongest desires of self. It was for food that Esau sold his birthright. It was to physical hunger -- the desire for food -- that Satan directed the first of the series of temptations to Christ when he was in the wilderness. Paul, that great apostle of power, declared that he was "in fastings often". (II Cor. 11:27.)

Food itself is not sinful. But if it is given undue importance, it becomes a god, and when it becomes a god, it becomes a SIN.

Paul warned his church at Philippi of some whom they might be tempted to follow, "they are the enemies of the cross of Christ: whose end is destruction, whose GOD IS THEIR BELLY, and whose glory is their shame, WHO MIND EARTHLY THINGS." Phil. 3:18, 19.

Many who desire the miracle working power of God in their lives today are hindered by the fact that they still would rather miss God's best for them than to miss a good meal.

How hard it was for me to remain on my knees in my closet of prayer when the good smell of food cooking began to filter in through the cracks around the door! And it was not until I resolutely turned my back upon the delicious stew, and went back to my closet without my dinner, that I heard the voice of God. It was only then that I proved to

God that he meant more to me than food -- that my belly was not my God.

Fasting itself has no power to accomplish miracles, unless it is done rightly. The Israelites of Isaiah's time cried out, "Wherefore have we fasted, and thou seest not?" (Isa. 58:3). God's reply, through his prophet, was, "Behold, in the day of your fast ye find pleasure, and exact all your labors. Behold ye fast for strife and debate, and to smite with the fist of wickedness: ye shall not fast as ye do this day, to make your voice to be heard on high." (v. 3, 4.) If our fasting is to help any about making our voice to be heard on high, it must be accompanied by a real heart searching, and seeking after God. It must include an enlarged vision of our responsibility to be our brother's keeper. Fasting must be done unselfishly, if it is to be done effectively. "Is not this the fast that I have chosen? to loose the bands of wickedness, to undo the heavy burdens, and to let the oppressed go free, and that ye break every yoke? Is it not to deal thy bread to the hungry, and that thou bring the poor that are cast out to thy house? when thou seest the naked that thou cover him; and that thou hide not thyself from thine own flesh?" (v. 6:7). When fasting is done God's way, he has given the promise, "Then shall thy light break forth as the morning, and thine health shall spring forth speedily; and thy righteousness shall go before thee; the glory of the Lord shall be thy reward. THEN SHALT THOU CALL, AND THE LORD SHALL ANSWER: thou shalt cry and he shall say, Here I am." V. 8, 9.

Jesus fasted, and expected that those who followed him would fast, but pointed out to his followers that not every fast was acceptable with God (See Matt. 6:16-18). Those who fasted boastfully were branded by him as HYPOCRITES. He declared that they received ALL of their reward in the admiration of those around them, who looked only upon the outward appearance. The fasting which he recommended was to be done privately -- a secret transaction between the individual and God. If possible, even the immediate family were not to be informed that a fast was in progress. When fasting is done this way, God will hear from heaven, and will reward you openly, by answering your prayer.

How much better to have people say, "That man has power with God. The sick are healed, the lame walk, the dumb speak, and the blind see when he prays," than to have them say, "That man is sure a pious man. He fasts three days of the week. He has completed a twenty one day fast, and is even now in the tenth day of a forty day fast."

Some fine people have been misled into wasted time and sacrifice, which brought no good to anyone because they became puffed up and did their fasting with a spirit of boastfulness. It is Satan's business to spoil all that we try to do for God. Let us be watchful in this matter, or else he will make useless one of our most effective weapons, the weapon of self-denial through fasting.

True fasting is a matter of giving God first place over all the demands of the self life. It goes deep into the personal life. Paul recommended that while husband and wife are each to consider his or her body the personal property of the other, and to be subject one to the other, seeking to please each other in every way possible, that it is wise that the Christian husband and wife set aside by agreement times when personal gratification is to be ruled out, in order that God may be FIRST, that he may occupy all their thoughts, that one or the other, or both together, may give themselves to fasting and prayer. God does not condemn marriage, nor the rightful relationship of husband and wife. But even this, which is rightfully yours, may, like our food, be set aside for a time of seeking God, with great profit.

The closer we walk to God, the greater will be the power in our lives. This closeness can be achieved in one way -- "Draw nigh to God and he will draw nigh to you." James 4:8.

Self-denial will many times take you out of the company which you would find most enjoyable. No doubt, the company you keep is good company. But if you are to have power with God, you must have fellowship with God. Fellowship with god's people is wonderful, and is needed by every Christian, especially those who are young in the Lord. But there is another fellowship which is even more necessary. "Truly our fellowship is with the Father, and with his Son Jesus Christ" I John 1:3.

Those who have power with God, and are bringing deliverance to the sick and suffering, and winning souls to Christ, are spending much time alone with God before they spend time with the people.

These things cannot be done in a moment. Power is the result of WAITING UPON THE LORD. Self says hurry. But self must be denied again. Pentecost followed ten days of waiting upon the lord. Daniel's vision of the last days followed 23 days of waiting. Because Moses had not learned to wait upon the Lord to know His method as well as His will, he had to wait forty years in exile before he was ready to do the work of deliverance which God had given him to do.

"Rest in the Lord, and wait patiently for him." Ps. 37:7.

Waiting is almost a lost art. Everything is done in a hurry. So many things require only the pushing of a button, but there is no button to push -- no magic formula -- no "royal road" -- to power with God. The man who has waited upon God commands the demon to depart, and the tormented one is free. The man who hasn't time to "waste" in waiting speaks the same words, seems to do the same things, but nothing happens. Waiting upon God is not wasted time, although it many times may seem to you as well as to others that you are doing nothing. Waiting on God includes fasting, prayer, and just plain waiting. When we pray, we talk to God but when you have prayed until there seems to be nothing more to say, then you need to wait for an answer. Let God speak to you.

Self is restless and impatient, always clamoring for action or for attention, or for gratification. Self is mindful of the things that are of this world, the things of the flesh. But "If any man will come after me, let him DENY HIMSELF." Luke 9:23.

Will you come after Him? Will you do the works He did? Then wait in His presence and let Him speak to your soul about the things of self which have not yet been denied. Let His life of self-denial be your pattern, and you are well on the way to sharing in His MIRACLE-WORKING POWER.

# CHAPTER 7

## THE CROSS

"If any man will come after me, let him deny himself, and
TAKE UP HIS CROSS DAILY and Follow me." Luke 9:23.

There will be very little gained by self-denial unless you
also take up your cross, and follow Jesus.

By the cross I mean that load, or burden, of pain or sorrow or sacrifice which could, if we choose, be laid aside, but
which is willingly carried or endured for the sake of others.
It is that which in the natural we WOULD lay aside, but
spurred on by the realization that there is no other way to
bring salvation, deliverance or healing to the lost, the sick
and the suffering, we willingly endure OUR CROSS.

"Looking unto Jesus -- who FOR THE JOY THAT WAS
SET BEFORE HIM, ENDURED THE CROSS, despising the
shame." Heb. 12:2. Jesus didn't have to endure the cross.
Even on the night when He was taken, He declared that
He could yet, at that late hour pray to the Father, and He
would send more than twelve legions of angels, to rescue
Jesus from such a fate. (See Matt. 26:53, 54.) He went to
the cross because he had purposed in His heart to fulfill
the scriptures, and to deliver the race of lost and sinful
men from the double curse of sin and sickness, by bearing
the stripes upon His back, and by being sacrificed, a lamb
without spot or blemish, upon THE CROSS.

Moses partook of this spirit, when he turned away from
the throne of Egypt to identify himself with his brethren, a
race of slaves, that he might through suffering and sacrifice
bring deliverance to them all. (See Heb. 11:24, 26.)

Paul demonstrated the same determination, when he left
his place in the Sanhedrin to join the despised and persecuted sect of Christians, that he might not be disobedi-
ent to the heavenly vision, and that he might bring deliverance to the Gentiles. He was following Jesus, BEARING

HIS CROSS, when he declared, "I go bound in the spirit unto Jerusalem, not knowing the things that shall befall me there: SAVE THAT THE HOLY GHOST WITNESSETH in every city, saying that BONDS AND AFFLICTIONS ABIDE ME. But none of these things MOVE ME, neither COUNT I MY LIFE DEAR unto myself, so that I might -- testify the gospel of the grace of God." Acts 20:22-24.

When Charles G. Finney left a promising law practice to enter the ministry -- an untried field for which he had no special training -- he took up his cross.

But taking up the cross is not enough. It must be taken up DAILY! It must be taken up willingly, and carried faithfully, without fretting. It is easy to make a consecration -- to take up the cross -- during the heat of an inspiring consecration call, but many fail to take it up again the next morning, or the next.

Christ never took a vacation from His cross. The cross even went with Him on His vacation! Although He stepped aside many times to rest, even then the burden was heavy upon Him when He sat down by the well in Samaria, weary and hungry, to rest while His disciples went into the city to buy food, He had time and strength to lead a soul to salvation, and to start a movement which later brought about the great revival, which swept most of Samaria into the Kingdom of God. (Acts 8.)

When He was confronted with one of the greatest griefs which came into His life as a man in the flesh, the sudden and violent death of His cousin and dear friend, John the Baptist, He thought to slip away alone for a little time. (See Matt. 14:13,14.) But the people observed His going, and followed Him even then. When He looked upon them, He was filled with compassion, His own grief was forgotten, and He took up His cross and went forth to heal their sick, and to minister to their needs.

The cross was not an accident which came to Him at the end of life. He was born, and lived and died under the shadow of the cross. He knew it was there all the time, but never once did He shun the cross. Never once did He fail to take up His cross DAILY. There was never a day that He could say, "This day is my own. I will go about my Father's business again tomorrow." Never an experience came into His life which He could say, "This is mine to enjoy. The people must wait until this is over. Then I will meet them and minister to their needs again." Even in His times of sorrow, He could not say, "My own grief is so great. It is no more than right that NOW I should be comforted. Let them minister unto me, now."

It was the night in which He was betrayed, when He knew that the time had come, and that the false disciple who would betray Him sat among those to whom He ministered, that He rose from the table to wash the feet of His disciples, demonstrating the thing which He had said before, "The Son of man came not to be ministered unto but to minister, and to give his life a ransom for many." Mark 10:45.

To the eyes of the world it would seem that it was only on that dark day of Calvary that "he bearing his cross went forth." John 19:16. But He had been bearing His cross as he went forth among the people, poor, despised, lonely, misunderstood -- willingly, that He might bring with Him many sons unto glory -- going about doing good and healing all that were oppressed of the devil.

The world may not see nor understand your cross and mine. But each of us has his own cross, God appointed, which he can bear or not as he sees fit. This is not sickness which we are helpless to lay aside. It is not those unpleasant circumstances of life which would be ours whether we serve God or not. It is that which we accept willingly, at personal sacrifice to ourselves, in order that we may be obedient to God and a blessing to others. Have you been complimenting yourself on your cross bearing, and is it just a matter of feeling sorry for yourself about the circumstances of your life? Have you willingly taken upon yourself the burdens and griefs and sorrows of others, that you might lift them, and be a blessing -- that you might bring salvation and deliverance to those in need?

You say you want God's miracle working power. Are you willing to pay the price? Are you willing to take up YOUR cross, DAILY, and follow Jesus all the way?

If you follow Christ fully, it will mean following Him to the place where he was filled with the Spirit, then on to the wilderness -- to the hours of fasting and prayer, to the hours of unappreciated service, through the misunderstandings and persecutions, the nights of watching alone in prayer. It will mean following Him into the garden -- bearing the burden of a lost world -- thinking someone nearby is sharing the load, only to find that all the rest have gone to sleep. Then away to the judgment hall -- false accusations, and unjust decisions. Now away to the whipping post, and the cat-o-nine tails -- the vinegar and the gall. It will allow no drawing back, even from the pain and suffering of the cross.

You may say, "That sounds like losing my life altogether."

Indeed it is. But Jesus said, "Whosoever will save his life shall lose it; but whosoever shall lose his life for my sake and the gospel's, the same shall save it." Mark 8:35.

This is life more abundant -- the life of POWER! The life of real satisfaction. The life of knowing that your living has not been in vain! Surely it is worth every sacrifice to know that we have followed in the steps of the son of God.

# CHAPTER 8

## ". . . I MUST DECREASE (John 3:30)

Under this heading, God began to deal with me about my pride. I had never felt that I was proud. If such a thought were suggested to my mind, either through preaching or by direct accusation, or even by the faithful dealing of the spirit, I, like so many others, excused myself by calling this thing "self respect," "poise," "good breeding," or "high-mindedness." But God called it "SIN." Prov. 21:4. "An high look, and a proud heart . . . is sin." Prov. 21:4.

In the searchlight of His presence, there was no use to try to make explanations. Like John of old, I was made to realize my utter dependence upon God, and how little my own efforts were worth. I was made to realize, as I had never realized before, that even the best of my efforts were so futile, that truly God must take full control of my life, and that, before that could happen, I (my own personality, talents, knowledge, or natural ability) MUST DECREASE in importance in my own opinion.

I have since discovered that the power and success of any man's ministry depends upon the amount, or greatness, of God in his life. The New Testament disciples depended entirely upon "The Lord working with them, and confirming the Word with signs following." Mark 16:20. They claimed no power nor holiness for themselves, although at their work of command, a man lame for forty years -- having to be carried by his friends to a place where he might beg for his living -- was instantly healed, so that he not only walked, but leaped and ran. (See Acts 3:2-8 and 12-16). These were the same men who had once rejoiced, saying, "Lord, even the devils are subject unto US through thy name." Luke 10:17. Now they have decreased in their own sight, and are ready for an increased ministry. Hear them say, "Why look ye so earnestly on us, as though by our own power or holiness we had made this man to walk? . . . His name through faith in his name hath made this man strong." Acts 3:12,16.

It is only as God increases in the life of one of His followers that power can increase, and this can never happen until SELF is decreased.

Oh that God's ministers -- yes, and laity as well -- could realize that it is "Not by MIGHT nor by POWER, but by my Spirit, saith the Lord of hosts." Zech. 4:6. The might and power here spoken of refer to man's might and power -- not to God's. To the natural and not to the supernatural. There are two sources of power. Many great church organizations today boast of their "power," "influence," or "popularity" in their community. Their power and influence are derived from the magnificence of their great church plants, their immense bank accounts, the efficiency of their organization, their numerical strength, and their connection with the "right" people -- those with wealth and influence in this world (though many of them do not so much as pretend ever to have been born again by the power of God, but only have joined the church as they would a social club.) Their fine talent, and soothing (spiritual sleep producing) worship services, their beautiful forms, all help to make them popular -- to give them power in a world of "religious," "respectable" sinners. It is from such as these that Paul has warned us (speaking as he was inspired by the Holy Ghost) that we must separate ourselves. "Having a form of Godliness, buy DENYING THE POWER THEREOF, from such turn away." II Tim. 3:5. These people would be greatly displeased if God should interrupt the controlled orderliness of one of their services by speaking out as He so often did in days gone by through one of His prophets, rebuking sin and calling them to lives of holiness and power. They make no plans, nor leave any room in their services, for the supernatural manifestation of the power of God.

True, there is a certain feeling of security and power, when we have achieved the building of a fine church edifice, have succeeded in bringing our organization to a state of good operating efficiency, have ceased to live in constant fear of not being able to meet our financial obligations, and are reaching the multitudes with the gospel. None of these things are wrong. We can gratefully thank God for them when they come our way. But all these things are noth-

ing -- they are only a lifeless shell -- if the SUPERNATU-
RAL POWER OF THE SPIRIT OF GOD is not there. They
are a mere tower of Babel, reaching up toward a sky that
is too far away, and doomed to failure and confusion, even
though they appear to be enjoying success.

How blessed to have talent, consecrated and used for the
glory of God. How good to have knowledge. What a comfort
to have proper accommodations. But the one thing that is
needful is the POWER OF GOD.

How many fine churches in our cities are finding their
auditoriums hard to fill, while men and woman stand in the
rain outside some great gospel tent, pitched on the edge of
town, trying to find some space to get inside, in order that
they may see what God is doing through His ministers who
have placed the power of God first in their lives -- who have
been willing to decrease that God might increase.

"Might," as Zechariah speaks of it, refers to the might of
man, as physical effort, natural ability, talents, forms, cer-
emonies, rituals, ordinances and programs.

When the supernatural is gone, man will substitute the
natural. He will substitute songs about the power of God
for the reality, laying more and more stress upon the har-
mony and musical flourishes, as the real power of God de-
creases. Thank God for good music, but in itself it IS NOT
THE POWER OF GOD! The might and the power of natural
man will never fulfill the great commission, and bring deliverance to the multitudes. Although God may use them
to some extent, with the anointing of the Spirit upon them,
they cannot be used as a SUBSTITUTE FOR THE SPIRIT!

Even beautifully outlined sermons, eloquently preached
by men of strong personality and charm, will never get the
job done alone. After all, even preaching is not our objec-
tive. It is merely a means to an end. If good sermonizing and
beautiful preaching could get the job done, it would have
been done long ago.

Oh that men would decrease!

Oh that they would realize that without God they are
NOTHING!

If preachers could only realize that it is not the beauty and
forcefulness of their preaching, altogether, which brings results, but the ANOINTING OF THE SPIRIT upon the sermon, and God in POWER in the man who does the preach-

ing. People need more than to hear a sermon. They need to FEEL SOMETHING while that sermon is being preached. It is the SPIRIT that causes people to FEEL the preaching.

Paul was not, like some of the other disciples, an ignorant and unlearned man. His was the best education available in his time. His speech to the men of Athens, on Mars Hill, is still recognized as one of the best classics of persuasive debate, and of homological and literary arrangement. (See Acts 17:22-31.) His background, education, and reputation among his fellows was such that he could declare, "I might also have confidence in the flesh. If any other man thinketh that he hath whereof he might trust in the flesh, I more." Phil. 3:4. But Paul turned it all aside. He was willing to decrease. "But what things were gain to me, those I counted loss for Christ." Phil. 3:7. Although, as we have already seen, Paul was capable of eloquent speech, he wrote to the Corinthians, "My speech and my preaching was NOT with enticing words of man's wisdom, BUT IN DEMONSTRATION OF THE SPIRIT AND OF POWER." I Cor. 2:4. In the next verse he tells us why he had laid aside his natural talents to depend upon the power of God and that alone. "That your faith should not stand in the wisdom of men, but in the power of God."

If the power of God were given its rightful place today, more people's faith would stand in the power of God. Not so many would be trusting in their CHURCH (instead of the lord) for salvation, and not so many would be carried away by some preacher's personality, so that they are of no use to God nor man unless they can work under His leadership.

Paul recognized the importance of the spirit upon his preaching. "Not that we are sufficient of ourselves to THINK ANYTHING as of our selves; but our sufficiency is of God; who also hath made us able ministers of the New Testament; NOT OF THE LETTER, BUT OF THE SPIRIT: FOR THE LETTER KILLETH, BUT THE SPIRIT GIVETH LIFE." II Cor. 3:5-6.

People today need LIFE (life cannot come without the Spirit). God will make us able ministers -- able to bring life and deliverance -- of the New Testament as we decrease to the extent that we place man with all his natural ability, all that calls attention to and glorifies man, in the background.

Although Paul was a man of more than usual knowledge,

due to his fine education and his richly varied experience, he was willing to cast it all aside, and to declare that he was "DETERMINED not to know ANYTHING among you save CHRIST." I Cor. 2:2.

Knowledge "puffeth up." I Cor. 1:8. Some people are of little use to God because they "know" too much. Paul speaks of some who are puffed up at the church at Corinth. (See I Cor. 4:18.) By this he meant they were "oversize," or needed to decrease, or be deflated. These seemed to be fine speakers, but Paul declared the test of what they were should be, not their speech, but POWER. "For the Kingdom of God is not in word, BUT IN POWER." Verse 20.

How easy it is to see that this is true! And how foolish we make ourselves appear many times, by trying to appear to be what we are not, because of pride!

Pride takes five forms. Pride of FACE. (How much better we DO look than those around about us!) Pride of PLACE. (Don't ask THAT of one in my POSITION!) Pride of RACE. (We come of an excellent family, you know, and must uphold the family honor at any cost.) Pride of PACE. (Everyone should be able to see that we are the most capable and efficient person available. No one else could keep up with us!) And then that last and WORST of all the forms of pride -- pride of GRACE! Proud of our spiritual accomplishments; proud of the length of our fasts; proud of visions and dreams and revelations; proud of the gifts we think we possess; feeling that we must be a special favorite with God; yes, even proud of our humility! Whatever form our pride may have taken, puffing us up like a toy balloon, the first thing that must be done, before we can have real power with God, is "I MUST DECREASE."

"Whosoever exalteth himself shall be abased; but he that humbleth himself shall be exalted." Luke 14:11.

"God resisteth the proud, but giveth grace unto the humble." James 4:6.

How, then, can you hope for God to work with you, confirming the Word with signs following, when God has said He is RESISTING YOU!

Yes, I must decrease. Only the gold must remain. All the dross must be taken away, and all the tin, before God can work with it as he desires to work. And how little there is left, when the dross is gone!

# CHAPTER 9

## "HE MUST INCREASE" (John 3:30)

Did you ever drive across the prairie, and note in the distance a mountain? At first sight the mountain seems very small. But as you drive on, and come closer to the mountain, you are astonished to see how rapidly it seems to grow. Really, the mountain isn't growing. It is still the same size as when you first observed it. The difference is that you have drawn closer to the mountain. This is exactly what takes place when God "increases." He is the same God to all men. But to some people, He seems to be a little, shriveled up, impotent God, who can scarcely be expected to do anything that really matters. The reason for this is that these people are living TOO FAR AWAY FROM HIM! This is why we are instructed, "Draw nigh to God." James 4:8.

God is far away from many people because they have allowed so many things to come in between. Some even draw nigh to God with their mouth, while their heart is far from Him. (Matt. 15:8.) Of these He says, "In vain do they worship me." The only way that it is possible to draw near to God, is to begin earnestly, with all your heart to search out those things which come between, and GET RID OF THEM!

Pride certainly will keep God at a distance. "The proud he knoweth AFAR OFF." Psalm 188:6. God cannot work WITH you when He is FAR FROM you. You must come to Him humbly.

Some have excused the lack of power in their lives, by saying, "The day of miracles is past. The church is established now, and it doesn't need miracles anymore." Nowhere does the scripture confirm any such thought. "Jesus Christ (is) the SAME, yesterday, today and forever." Heb. 13:8.

Behold, the Lord's hand is not shortened, that it cannot save; neither his ear heavy, that it cannot hear: BUT YOUR INIQUITIES HAVE SEPARATED BETWEEN YOU AND YOUR

GOD." Isa. 59:1, 2. Don't blame God for your lack of power. Put the blame squarely where it belongs. YOU are too far from God, because there are too many iniquities (sins) in between.

Friends and loved ones may come between. Jesus said, "He that loveth father or mother more than me is not worthy of me: and he that loveth son or daughter more than me is not worthy of me." Matt. 10:37.

The cares of life may come between, as weeds choking out a crop, making it unfruitful. Some give all their thought to the things of this life, as though they would live here forever. God cannot work with such as these. To be near to the heart of God, and to feel the pulse beat of His compassion for the lost, and the suffering, one must have a constant realization of the shortness of life, and the inevitability of eternity.

Some are kept at a distance from God by lack of appreciation. Praise is lacking in their lives.

Real appreciation for what God IS and what He has done, will bring forth praise. Praise brings us into the very presence of God. "Enter into his gates with thanksgiving, and into his courts with praise." Ps. 100:4.

Some who read this book, may not know that God desires to be so near to his people, as to send his HOLY SPIRIT to take up his abode not simply near, but WITHIN the child of God. When you have opened your heart and allowed the Spirit of God to fill you, baptize you, taking possession of every part of your body, you will find him much nearer than ever before. He will be a much greater God to you, than you have ever known. Then as he is allowed to continue to dwell in you richly, teaching and guiding you day by day, into a closer relationship with the father, and into a more pure life of holiness, the greatness of God will become more and more apparent. He will increase in your life.

The more you come to know Him, by walking by his side day by day, and the more you feed upon his word, the more he will increase in your sight. All that we know of God, we know by faith. "Faith cometh by hearing, and hearing by the word of God." Rom. 10:17. Feed upon the Word of God. It is strange, but some even hope to have power with God who pay very little heed to the word of God. He will not honor with his presence those who dishonor his word.

It is the Word of God which will help us to cleanse from our lives the SINS which stand between. "Wherewithal shall a young man cleanse his way? By taking heed thereto according to thy word." Psalm 119:9.

In dealing with me about this matter, God made it very plain to me that if these things were allowed to persist in my life, if sin were tolerated and allowed to remain, God would continue to be at a distance from me. He would be so far away, that he would be to me only the little, meaningless God whom so many others profess to serve. The only way that God could increase in my life to the point where he would be working through me in power, was for me to keep everything out from between me and God. The only way he could remain the great "I AM" in my own experience, was for me to continually walk in the light of his word, by the power of his spirit, DECREASING day by day, becoming more and more absorbed in Him who must INCREASE.

He MUST increase! Not could increase. Not might increase. He MUST increase. He must increase in glory, and majesty and power. He must increase in control of my life.

"I am crucified with Christ. Nevertheless I live; YET NOT I, BUT CHRIST LIVETH IN ME." Gal. 2:20.

"Fill me with thy spirit, till all the world may see, Not me, but Jesus only, shining out through me."

# CHAPTER 10

## IDLE WORDS AND FOOLISH TALKING

"Every idle (unprofitable) word that men shall speak, they shall give account thereof in the day of judgment." Matt. 12:36.

Nothing more quickly and thoroughly reveals the lack of real spirituality than does foolish talking, jesting, and IDLE WORDS. There is nothing that will more surely label the shallow Christian as one who has no concern for others, nor any burden for the lost and suffering than his perpetual flow of foolish talking, and nonsensical joking. Although in the eyes of many, this seems to be a small matter, there are few spiritual diseases more devastating, nor more contagious.

God classes foolish talking along with some very unattractive companions, -- "But fornication, and all uncleanness, or covetousness, let it not be once named among you, as becometh saints: neither filthiness, nor FOOLISH TALKING, nor JESTING, which are not convenient: but rather giving of thanks." Eph. 5:3,4.

Jesus himself declared, "--Evil thoughts, adulteries, fornications, murders, thefts, covetousness, wickedness, deceit, lasciviousness, an evil eye, blasphemy, pride, FOOLISHNESS: all these EVIL THINGS come from within, and DEFILE the man." Mark 7:21-23. Foolishness then will defile a man, the same as fornication! There are many who would never kill nor steal, but will even enter the pulpit, and publicly and unashamed, reveal through their words that they are defiled within. I have never yet found a man whom the Lord is using mightily for the deliverance of the sick and sinful whose mouth is filled with foolishness. They may entertain the people, and get a few hearty laughs in response to their jokes and nonsense, but when it comes to really being able to bring deliverance, or to bring a help and blessing

when a real need arises, THEY HAVEN'T GOT THE GOODS!
They may even try at times to put off the usual character
of lightness for a little while, and to preach or teach about
deep things, but to those who hear them there is no ring of
sincerity, no real persuasion that they speak as the oracles
of God. They are like sounding brass, or a tinkling cymbal.

I do not wish to infer that God's people should go around
with a long face all the time, having no joy. God's people
are the happiest people in the world. God has commanded,
"Rejoice evermore." I Thes. 5:13. God's people are expected
to be so happy that they will shout, sing, clap their hands,
dance, laugh, and even leap for joy. A few scriptures which
show these things are the following:

"Make a JOYFUL NOISE unto the Lord, all ye lands. Serve
the Lord with GLADNESS: come before his presence with
SINGING." Ps. 100:1, 2.

"O CLAP YOUR HANDS, all ye people: SHOUT unto God
with the voice of triumph." Ps. 47:1. "Let them praise his
name in the DANCE: let them SING praises unto him with
the TIMBREL and HARP." Ps. 149:3. "David DANCED before the Lord with all his might." II Sam. 6:14.

"Then was our mouth filled with LAUGHTER, and our
tongue with SINGING: then said they among the heathen,
The Lord hath done great things for us; whereof we are
GLAD." Ps. 126:2, 3.

"Rejoice in that day, and LEAP FOR JOY." Luke 6:23. For
the Joy of the Lord is thy strength." Neh. 8:10.

The Christian who doesn't have JOY is a weak Christian,
a poor representative of the faith he claims, and will probably soon be completely backslidden, and seeking his joy
somewhere else.

This joy which brings strength is rejoicing in the Lord. It
is not rejoicing in the power of our own strength, nor of our
own wit. "But now rejoice ye in your boastings: all such rejoicing is evil." James 3:2.

Many who are guilty of the sin of foolish, excessive, and
unprofitable talking will at first be tempted to brand me a
fanatic, and to rise to the defense of their pet sin. They will
declare that it is a mistake to take things too seriously. For
this, they can find no scriptural defense. The rescuing of
the lost, and deliverance of the suffering, is a serious matter, requiring the whole heart and mind of the one who is

consecrated to the task. Many have reserved the right to talk as much, and in whatever manner, they choose. They would rather have their jokes, foolish jesting and nonsense than to have the power of God in their lives. If this is your case, God will have to go on without YOU.

God has chosen to work through the spoken word of representatives in the world. When Jesus was here, he said to his disciples, "The WORDS that I speak unto you, THEY ARE SPIRIT, AND THEY ARE LIFE." John 6:63. What are your words?

James compares the speech coming out of our mouths to water coming from a fountain. (James 3:10,11.) He insists that a fountain should give forth the same kind of water all the time -- not sweet water part of the time, and bitter water part of the time. Then he adds, "Who is a wise man and endued with knowledge among you? Let him show out of a good CONVERSATION his works with meekness of wisdom." James 3:13.

"Let no corrupt communication proceed out of your mouth, BUT THAT WHICH IS GOOD TO THE USE OF EDIFYING." Eph. 4:29.

Words which are not good to the use of edifying are IDLE (vain, empty, or unprofitable) words. They are WASTED words. God has given to the believer's WORD an authority and power which makes it precious. Precious things should not be wasted.

Jesus said, "Whosoever (that means you!) shall SAY unto this mountain, be thou removed, and be thou cast into the sea; and shall not doubt in his heart, but shall believe that those things which he SAITH shall come to pass, he shall have WHATSOEVER HE SAITH." Mark 11:23. This gives to US the power to speak with authority, even to the extent of controlling inanimate things. This is the same power which Jesus used when he spoke to the wind and the sea, and the storm was gone. (Mark 4:39.) It is the same power which Moses used when he spoke to the rock in the desert, and water gushed forth. (Num. 20:8.) Joshua used the same power when he commanded the sun and the moon to stand still. (Joshua 10:12, 13.) Jesus demonstrated the use of this power when he spoke to the fig tree, saying, "No man eat fruit of thee hereafter forever." (Mark 11:14.) He told the tree to die, AND it died! It was on this occasion that he expressly delegated this same power and authority to ANY who BELIEVE.

It is to men and women whose words can be with such power -- whose spoken words can bring deliverance from every oppression of Satan -- salvation for the soul and healing for the body -- that Jesus warned that IDLE, WASTED, WORDS should be brought into judgment. Words which should have been life and deliverance! Words which should have been bread to starving souls! But words which were nothing but chaff! In the face of a world of dying, starving souls and suffering humanity, withholding the one source of life and deliverance, and offering stones for bread! Sending forth from the fountain which should give forth the PURE WATER OF LIFE a stream of froth and foolishness, which is, if not poisonous, utterly unattractive and unprofitable! What will you say to the judge in that day, when our deeds and WORDS are judged by the standard of the word of God, in which we are exhorted, "If any man SPEAK, let him SPEAK AS THE ORACLES (utterance or speech) OF GOD." I Peter 4:11.

Those who insist upon having their foolishness at any cost, are so like the group of young ladies seen in a vision by a consecrated saint of God, who were too busy making daisy chains to warn the people who were hurrying by that their steps were leading to an awful precipice, where they would quickly fall over, and be dashed to death upon the rocks below. This is far from the spirit of Christ, who HAD COMPASSION UPON THE MULTITUDES.

I do not intent to infer that there is no place for humor in the conversation of the Christian, or even in the preaching of the Word. Many times, our speech or preaching can be humorous, and yet sanctified. Often, a bit of humor, especially when used to illustrate a point, can be very profitable, in arousing the attention and interest of the hearers, and in driving home the message of the gospel, so that souls are aroused and turned to God. So used, it is NOT idle, nor unprofitable.

The reason so many Christians speak so many idle words, is that they speak SO MANY WORDS! They talk so much that they have no time to think, and no time to listen to the voice of God. Foolish words come so easily. We do not even have to think of them. We can listen to any conversation, anywhere, and come away with a large supply of them which can be produced by repetition. The spirit of the age is an ever increasing spirit of levity, which makes serious thinking difficult for both sinner and saint. It is typified by the oft repeated saying, "Don't take life too seriously. After all you'll never get out of it alive." In such an age it takes real effort and consecration to "Study to be quiet", and to wait before God long enough to have words to speak which are the words of God, and which can have power. But the wise man will do it. "He that hath knowledge, spareth his words." Prov. 17:27. "But the mouth of fools FEEDETH ON FOOLISHNESS." Prov. 15:14.

"In the multitude of words there wanteth not sin." Prov. 10:19.

A fool's voice is known BY MULTITUDE OF WORDS." Eccl. 5:3.

Holiness is necessary for power, as has already been shown in previous chapters of this book. And holiness is not complete until it has also taken possession of the tongue. "But as he which hath called you is holy, so be ye holy IN ALL MANNER OF CONVERSATION." I Pet. 1:15.

I beseech you, brethren, for the sake of the lost and suffering who will never find deliverance UNLESS YOU MAKE YOURSELF READY TO TAKE IT TO THEM, give this matter your prayerful consideration. Consecrate yourself to God afresh. Present to him YOUR BODY, a living sacrifice, AND DO NOT FORGET NOR NEGLECT TO INCLUDE YOUR TONGUE, YOUR LIPS, YOUR VOICE!"

"Let your speech be always with grace, seasoned with salt." Col. 4:6.

"Keep that which is committed to thy trust (the power to speak in God's stead, and bring deliverance), avoiding profane (not holy) and vain (empty, worthless) babblings." I Tim. 6:20.

It is my prayer that all who read this book will put all on the altar, and get in a place where they can carry a burden for the lost and suffering: that they will cast aside ALL those things which hinder the power of God in their lives. God can go on without you. But if YOU go on with God, you must go His way. Put foolishness aside NOW! Get out of the eddy and into the stream of God's power.

The PROMISES are for you, if you will only believe them, meet God's conditions, and PAY THE PRICE.

# CHAPTER 11

## PRESENT YOUR BODY

I beseech you therefore, brethren, by the mercies of God, that ye present your bodies a living sacrifice, holy, acceptable unto God, which is your reasonable service." Rom. 12:1.

God has never made it a habit to use things THAT DO NOT BELONG TO HIM. He uses those things which are yielded to him. Things that are CONSECRATED. THINGS THAT ARE SANCTIFIED -- SET APART FOR HIS USE. Do you want God to USE YOU? Then you must PRESENT YOUR BODY. It must be completely yielded and surrendered to God. A body that is not completely yielded and surrendered to God is still more or less domineered by Satan, or by self.

Many no doubt have, at special times, after a fashion, presented their bodies to the Lord for his use in stretching forth the borders of his Kingdom. But it is obvious from the fact that they are not being used, that many of those who have presented themselves have NOT BEEN ACCEPTED.

God has not refused them because laborers are not needed. Christ himself gave us the command to pray that more laborers would be sent forth because "THE HARVEST TRULY IS PLENTEOUS, BUT THE LABORERS ARE FEW." Matt. 9:37.

God has not refused them because of their handicaps, for he has often used those who seemed to have little natural qualification. Peter and John, men greatly used of God, were "unlearned and ignorant men" Acts 4:13. Moses was "slow of speech." "Not many wise men after the flesh, not many noble, are called; BUT GOD HATH CHOSEN the foolish things of the world to confound the wise; and God hath chosen the weak things of the world to confound the things which are mighty; and the base things of the world and things which are despised --." I Cor. 1:27, 28. You think you are handicapped? All are handicapped in some way.

A young man was saved, and desired to give his testimony in a street meeting that others might know the matchless grace of God, but he could not give his testimony because of his stammering. Yet his love for God, and his desire to work for God drove him to his knees, and out again before the people. God heard his cry and helped him. He became a great preacher of the gospel and for many years was annually the chief speaker at a large camp meeting in New York.

To be an acceptable sacrifice, your body need not be strong nor beautiful. David Brainerd, great missionary to the American Indians in the early days, was declared to be dying of tuberculosis. He was warned that the only chance for him to live more than a few weeks was complete rest. But he brought what he had and made an acceptable sacrifice. He fell on his face before God, crying, "Give me souls or take my soul!" Then he rose up and went out to many years of fruitful ministry among the people God had laid upon his heart, and won thousands of them to Christ.

The only reason God has refused some is that THEY ARE NOT ACCEPTABLE! God makes just two requirements for an "acceptable sacrifice".

It must be HOLY. And it must be HIS.

That which is not holy is an abomination to God. A sacrifice brought in and offered to God for his service, which is defined by the habits and sins of the world is no more acceptable to him than the pig offered upon the sacred altar of the temple at Jerusalem by Antiochus Epiphanies. IT WILL NOT BE ACCEPTED.

That which is HIS must be his not only on Sunday and on prayer meeting night, but seven days and nights EVERY WEEK. It must be presented with NO STRINGS ATTACHED. It must be given with the heart cry, "I renounce all authority over this gift, now and forever. It is yours to use, to set aside, or to destroy. Whatever you choose to do with it, it is yours. If it is only a hidden ministry of prayer and personal testimony -- YES, LORD. If it is in my own home town, that is all right. If it takes me far across the sea, to strange lands and unfriendly peoples -- if it is to die for my faith, at the hands of persecutors, or to live under conditions that are worse than death -- still this body is yours. Do with it as you please. Feed it or starve it. Chill it in the far North, or let it suffer with the heat of Africa. Exalt it or humiliate it. It is all yours."

Acceptable consecration is like handing God a blank paper, with your name signed at the bottom, and saying, "Fill it in any way you want. That shall be my contract for the use of my entire life."

This sacrifice is not complete with merely saying yes or no to certain callings or requests of the spirit of God AFTER THEY HAVE BEEN GIVEN. It is the whole hearted determination to do the will of God ALL MY LIFE, no matter what it may be, nor what it may cost. It is the realization that "Ye are not your own."

You may find a small measure of power, and a small measure of blessing, when you have made a small measure of sacrifice. But if you would really experience the free flow of GOD'S MIRACLE WORKING POWER, you MUST present your body, a living sacrifice, HOLY, ACCEPTABLE UNTO GOD.

# CHAPTER 12

## A PARTAKER OF HIS DIVINE NATURE

"Whereby are given unto us exceeding great and precious promises that by these you might be PARTAKERS OF DIVINE NATURE." I Pet. 1:4.

God IS power. There is no power for good in this world except that power come from God. Christ himself, when he came into this world in the flesh, declared that he derived his power from God. "I do NOTHING of myself." John 8:28. "The Son CAN do nothing of himself." John 5:19. "I am in the father, and the Father in me. The Words that I speak unto you, I speak not of myself: but the FATHER THAT DWELLETH IN ME, HE DOETH THE WORKS." John 14:10.

After making the emphatic statement of John 14:10, Christ turned to his disciples with a promise -- "Verily, verily, I say unto you, He that believeth on me, THE WORKS THAT I DO SHALL HE DO ALSO; and greater works than these shall he do; because I go unto my Father." John 14:12. But, even as his own work and fruitfulness was conditioned upon his abiding in the

Father, our work and fruitfulness was conditioned upon our abiding in him. "Abide in me, and I in you. As the branch cannot bear fruit of itself, except it abide in the vine; no more can ye, except ye abide in me." Jn. 15:4. "Without ME YE can do nothing." Jn. 15:5.

The branch is PARTAKER of the nature of the vine. The same sap flows through it. The texture of the wood is the same. The leaves are the same. The fruit is the same. The bark is the same. IT IS PART OF THE VINE! So long as it remains in the vine, it can do whatever the vine can do. But whenever it is separated -- cut off -- from the vine, it can no longer do what the vine can do. The life giving sap ceases to flow through the branch, and it is no longer partaker of the nature of the vine. For it is the nature of the vine to BRING

FORTH FRUIT, and that the severed branch can never do.

Branches can be "cut off", and they can be grafted.

We, as sinners saved by grace, are compared in God's word to the branches of a wild olive tree, grafted in. Having been grafted in, we become PARTAKERS of the "root and fatness" of the olive tree. (Rom. 11:17.) If a graft is WELL MADE, so that nothing comes between and interferes with the flow of the sap into the new limb, it very soon comes to LOOK AND ACT like the other parts of the tree.

What a privilege to be made a partaker of the divine nature of God -- to LOOK in such a way that those who see us will realize that we have been with Jesus, and to ACT so much like him that the works he did WE DO ALSO!

We can only be partakers of this divine nature by his PROMISES, through faith in his promises. We partake of the divine nature in its effectiveness as we exercise the gifts of the spirit, and in its essence as we show forth the fruits of the spirit. It is in the exercising of the gifts of the Spirit that God shows forth through us his MIRACLE WORKING POWER. "Having then gifts differing -- whether prophecy, let us prophecy ACCORDING TO THE PROPORTION OF FAITH." Rom. 12:6. This is the secret of whatever work we are able to do for God. It is done ACCORDING TO THE PRO-PORTION OF FAITH. We are partakers of the divine nature ACCORDING TO THE PROPORTION OF FAITH. Little faith, the branch is barely alive, the sap barely getting through, a few green leaves making promise that fruit might come. More faith, more of the divine nature, fruitfulness. Much faith, ABUNDANT LIFE, the life giving sap flowing freely to every part of the branch, the weight of the fruit bowing it almost to the ground!

He who is a partaker of the divine nature of Christ will be a partaker of his nature of meekness and humility. The love and compassion of the nature of Christ will be appar-ent in all the activities and contacts of his daily life. The gentleness and kindness, the goodness, the longsuffering, and peace. The joy in service, the self-denial (temperance) -- all these will be a part of the life of the person who is a partaker of the divine nature. These may not have been part of your nature before Christ came to dwell in you, but when you have become a partaker of his nature, these things will replace the former things, which were your OWN CARNAL

NATURE.

Then when you are a partaker of his divine nature, there will be a wisdom which comes from following the leading of the Spirit. Not the wisdom which is purely natural, nor a wisdom gained merely from observation, but a spirit led wisdom which is incomprehensible to those who do not understand the leading of the spirit. There will be knowledge which comes to your mind out of the knowledge stored in the mind of God. Things which you need to know, but have no other way of knowing, God himself can and will reveal them unto you. There will be POWER, for God IS power! Miracles and Signs will follow. The sick will be healed, the lame will walk, cancers will vanish at your command. The blind will see, the deaf hear. Secrets of people's hearts will, when necessary, be made manifest. Souls will be stirred from the sleep of spiritual death, and brought as new creatures into the kingdom. Yea, even some whose physical lives are gone, may be brought again from the dead, in the will of God.

God plays no favorites. The same price of power stands to all. And the same power is available to ALL WHO WILL PAY THE PRICE!

To everyone who, by faith, will take his "exceeding great and precious promises" for himself, believing with all his heart that GOD MEANT EXACTLY WHAT HE SAID, thus becoming a PARTAKER OF HIS DIVINE NATURE, the door is open to new adventures of faith, beyond your wildest dreams!

# CHAPTER 13

## PERSONAL THINGS

These are the eleven POINTS. I trust that God has made them live to you, and used them, as I have told them to you, to bring you closer to himself and into a position to have THE MIRACLE WORKING POWER OF GOD in your own life.

No doubt you have wondered many times, what were those two things which were so personal. This chapter will deal with this matter of "Personal Things". I cannot tell you what they were, for deep in my heart, I feel the Lord would not have me to do so. But as you read this book, read the Bible, and wait before the Lord in prayer, I am sure that you, too, will find some "Personal Things".

I pray that you may have been inspired to PRESS TO-WARD THE MARK for the prize of the high calling of God in Jesus Christ." Phil. 3:14. To keep on pressing, until God is working in your life in Miracle Working Power. To strive earnestly for perfection in the sight of God, and to be in his perfect will.

"Let us therefore, as many as be perfect be thus minded; and if in anything ye be otherwise minded, GOD SHALL REVEAL EVEN THIS UNTO YOU." Phil. 3:15.

This is his promise. You need never know what were those things which God pointed out to me as being my OWN, PERSONAL, pet sins, which had to be pointed out by name. But you do need to recognize your own pet sins, which keep you from having the power God wants you to have!

I have found in my travels as an evangelist, as well as in experiences gained in pastorates, that most people have a pet sin which they have pampered and petted, and developed, for years. Paul terms it, "The sin which doth so easily beset us." (Heb. 12:1.), your "besetting sin". He also says it must be LAID ASIDE if we are to gain the prize at the end of the race. "Let us lay aside every weight and the sin which doth so easily beset us, and let us run with patience the race that is set before us."

Many good people, who COULD HAVE BEEN effective Christian workers have become so discouraged by the excess weights which they have failed to lay aside, that they have long ago dropped out of the race, and have become skeptics, even questioning the words of Jesus, concerning "signs following", and the power which God promised to the believer, that he should do the works which Christ did. Many over the land today are even now on the verge of giving up all hope of ever knowing God in the fullness of His power. DO NOT GIVE UP. Get alone with God. Seek him earnestly, whatever the cost may be, until he has revealed to you YOUR PET SIN. Until he has shown you what in your life needs cleansing before you can experience the power of God.

A rich young ruler once came to Jesus, anxious to know what was wrong with his religious experience. He was so anxious that he literally came RUNNING, and FELL DOWN at the master's feet. When he inquired, 'What must I do --?" Jesus replied, "one thing thou lackest --." Christ then put his finger upon the young man's pet sin, and instructed him how to get rid of it. (See Mk. 10:21.) As you seek the Lord, remember that he is always faithful to put his finger on your pet sin, as he did for the rich young ruler. Failure to place that sin upon the altar will cause you, too, to go away GRIEVED, just as he did. When God speaks to you, no matter how small the voice, OBEY! Get rid of that PET SIN and go on with God!

Your pet sin is the sin that you do not want the preacher to preach about. It is the sin for which you are always ready to make an excuse.

It is the sin which, although you would not admit that it is sin, you prefer to do it when you think no one is going to find out.

It is the sin which leads you captive most easily.

It is the sin which you are always ready to defend.

It is the sin which causes the clouds of doubt and remorse to cross your spiritual sky, whenever you really feel the need to contact God.

It is the sin which you are most unwilling to give up.

It is the sin which you think is so small that God should scarcely be able to see it, yet so large that you are sure you could never live without it.

Yet it is the sin which must be FLUNG (Weymouth) aside or else you must drop out of the race. And, last, it is the sin you are continually trying to make yourself believe is an infirmity. Be honest with yourself, and call it SIN! Do not call jealousy, watchfulness. If you are covetous, don't call yourself economical. If you are guilty of the sin of pride, don't dress it up as self-respect. If you are one of those who constantly exaggerates (stretches the truth), you may as well admit that that which is not the truth is a LIE! Are you bound by a perverse (stubbornly wrong) demon? Be careful, or you will pride yourself in being very firm. If your besetting sin is lust, don't excuse yourself that you are just oversexed by nature. Don't call criticizing, the gift of discernment, nor claim to be a good judge of human nature. Are you fretful, and complaining? Satan will tell you that you are nervous, and in your condition, this fretfulness can't be helped.

Come on, friend. Be honest with yourself and God. Call it exactly what it is. If it is sin, call it sin, and get down before God and ask him to set you free and make you an overcomer.

No doubt many excuse themselves for their many "little" sins by pointing out, "Why everyone does that! Remember, you can't pattern your life after other people's mistakes. How do you know that God has not spoken to them many times about this very thing? Don't be as guilty of disobedience as they.

And what if he didn't speak to them about it? Remember the exhortation of Jesus to Peter when he enquired what would be required of another disciple. "What is that to thee? FOLLOW THOU ME." John 21:22.

Consecration has much to do with personal things. It is the putting off, out of our lives, the hundred and one little things that in themselves may not be sin, but which if they are allowed to remain, take the place that Christ should take. As an example, many professing Christians admit that they do not read their Bible as much as they should. They declare that they are so busy, they just don't have time to read it. Yet these same people have time to read all the daily and Sunday comic strips, many magazines and stories.

There is but one conclusion. These comics, magazines, and stories are more important to them than the word of God. They have crowded out Christ from his rightful place in these people's lives. Some of this reading might be of such a nature as to be actually sinful in itself, but much of it is rather harmless, except for the fact that it HAS CROWDED OUT CHRIST. Thousands of those who profess to be believers in the Lord Jesus Christ today would have more power in their lives if the time they spend in listening to the ball games and "soap operas", and "perpetual emotion dramas" were spent listening to the voice of God, alone in the closet of prayer. These are some of the "little foxes that spoil the vines", destroying the tender grapes and robbing God's people of fruitfulness.

How much more powerful would be the lives of many, if the time they spend in front of their television sets (of course, they wouldn't go to a theater!) watching the wrestling matches were spent down upon their knees wrestling against Satan -- against the principalities and powers and the rulers of darkness of this world, and against spiritual wickedness in high places. (Eph. 6:12).

It isn't always the harsh, gross sins that stand between man and God. In fact, the sins which seem to keep most people from the best that God has for them, are the things that "everybody does". I'd go a little slow in saying "everybody". Those who are carrying a burden for this lost, sin sick, Christ-rejecting, hell-bound world, those who are doing the works which Christ promised them they should do, who have the signs following their ministry, and who are bringing deliverance to the needy, have long ago laid those things aside. You may be right in saying, "NEARLY everyone in my church does it." But don't forget that while they are doing these things, they, too, are wondering why they do not have the MIRACLE WORKING POWER OF GOD, and do not exercise the gifts of the spirit. Many of the same crowd wonder if they are ready for the rapture!

Many times I have made altar calls after preaching on the coming of the Lord, for those who do not know that they are ready for the coming of Christ. At such times I have been surprised at the great number of people who raised their hands WHO PROFESSED TO BE SAVED, AND EVEN SPIRIT FILLED, PEOPLE! It is evident that many so called saints today are not even living a sufficiently victorious life to know they are ready for the rapture. These CANNOT HAVE CONSISTENT MIRACLE WORKING POWER! They may have a prayer answered now and then, but the times in which we live, and the condition of the world about us demand more than that. YOU CANNOT PATTERN YOUR LIFE AFTER THIS CROWD. There is one whose life is worthy to be a pattern for ours. That one is JESUS.

Some may be unwilling to accept the teachings of holiness found in this book. I have no apology to make, if you do not. I quote Jesus all the way through the book. If you disagree with him, it is time you had better take stock of yourself, and begin to agree with God. "Can two walk together except they be agreed?" Amos 3:3. If you expect to walk with God, and to have power in your life to work the works of God, IT IS TIME TO AGREE WITH GOD. When you fully agree with God, this will put you in disagreement with some others. It is better to agree with God, even if in doing so one must disagree with others whose opinions he formerly honored and valued. Too many today are living to please others, and self, rather than the Lord.

There comes a time in the life of every person when he is at the fork in the road. Men of God and of Power throughout the ages have come to this fork in the road, and have chosen the way that seemed hard and that brought persecution, suffering and POWER because of God's approval. Others have come to the fork in the road, and have chosen the way that seemed more attractive, and have found that it led to prosperity, popularity, and destruction. Picture Lot of old, as he pondered the best course to take. There was the watered valley, with the prosperous city of Sodom at its center. Surely this was an easier way than to turn to the lonely rough hills. He felt sure he could go among those people in the valley, mind his own affairs, and not partake of their sins. And even at the end, God still accounted him as a "righteous man", but he had no power for God. Not even so much as to be able to rescue his own married daughters from the destruction of Sodom, for he seemed to them as one that mocked. (Gen. 19:14).

This way is still open to those who choose it. But thank God for the better way. It is open too. It is marked by the feet of such men as Moses, who "By faith -- when he was come to years, refused to be called the son of Pharaohs daughter; choosing rather to suffer affliction with the people of God, than to enjoy the pleasures of sin for a season." Heb. 11:24, 25.

And of Joseph, who when he came to this same fork in the road, chose to keep himself pure, although it meant spending years in an Oriental dungeon, with no assurance (except in his soul) that he would ever be released. And of Daniel, who as a slave boy, declined to drink the king's wine, and who later kept his appointment with God, although it meant a trip to the lion's den.

These men said no to Satan that they might say yes to God. Moses weighed the pleasures and treasures of Egypt against the call of God, and decided in favor of the call of God. He knew that the pleasures of sin could only last for a season. He esteemed the reproach of Christ GREATER RICHES! He had a true sense of values. How many today do not. They seem to think the greater riches are those of Egypt -- Hollywood, Broadway, or Wall Street. It is impossible to say yes to God until we have first said no to the things of the world.

Those whose minds are set upon worldly things would quickly have advised Moses that he was making a very unwise choice, giving up so much for so little. But Moses received his reward. He became a FRIEND OF GOD -- one who talked with God face to face. His face shone so with the brightness of the glory of God, that the people could not even bear to look upon his face. And working hand in hand with God, he led three million people out of bondage into liberty, and saw them miraculously delivered time after time, and kept by the hand of God so that "There was not one feeble person in all their tribes." Ps. 105:37. Truly this is the reward which we seek today -- that we might be enabled to bring salvation and deliverance to the people. And God is giving that reward to many today who have heard his voice and obeyed his call! Who have said no to the world and yes to God!

God, in days gone by, "Sought for a man, that should make up the hedge and stand in the gap before (him) for the land that (He) might not destroy it." Ezek. 22:30-31. God is looking for such men today. God's holiness demands that he send judgment upon a wicked world. Only the presence of the righteous in the world holds back the floods of judgment. Moses stood in the gap for the children of Israel, and their lives were spared. (See Exodus 32:10, 11) Abraham stood in the gap for Lot and his family, when they were in Sodom. And Lot, had he gathered around him a group of righteous people, saved from their sinfulness through his testimony and influence, could have stood in the gap for the entire city of Sodom. (Gen. 18:23, 19:15.)

The generation in which we live is a wicked generation, similar to those among whom Lot lived. It is a sick sin, judgment bound generation. The wrath of God is already pronounced against ALL who partake of the wickedness of the world in such an age as this. But God does not take pleasure in pouring out judgment. Now as in days gone by, he looks for A MAN -- any man, or a woman will do -- who can and will love the people enough to make the sacrifices necessary to stand in the gap -- to hold back the storm of judgment -- to stand with the storm beating upon his back while he raises his voice long and loud, pleading with the people to flee from the wrath to come.

The world is setting the stage for the last great scene of the great story, "The History of Man upon the Earth." Soon the curtain will rise upon that last scene, the terrible tribulation period, when the wrath of God will be poured out without measure upon a wicked world from which the last righteous person has been hastily snatched away. The clouds are gathering, the lightening is flashing, the thunder rolls -- gusts of the wind which precede the storm can be felt with ever increasing frequency and force.

"Lift up your eyes and look on the fields; for they are white already to harvest." John 4:35. As never before, it is URGENT that the servants of God should place the work of the harvest ahead of everything else -- that they should "WORK, for the night COMETH WHEN NO MAN CAN WORK!" It is a time when ALL THE POWER OF GOD PROVIDED needs to be brought into use to save as much as possible of the precious harvest before the storm breaks. This is a time when YOU AND I need to find the gap in which God would have us stand, and STAND THERE, faithful.

How sad it was when God looked, hopefully, for a man to stand in the gap and he had to continue his statement, "I found NONE. Therefore have I poured out mine indignation upon them. I have consumed them with the fire of My wrath."

God is still looking for MEN TO STAND IN THE GAP! He is still looking for laborers for the harvest. He offers the same wages -- the same rewards -- for those who will come at this last hour, as for those who have borne the heat of the battle. All he asks is a quick response to his call, and faithfulness in carrying it out. Will you say "YES" to this call of God? Will you give him your ALL? Will you accept his BEST -- the MIRACLE WORKING, SOUL SAVING POWER OF GOD, for the deliverance of the lost, the sick and the suffering?

Much has been done for the deliverance of humanity by holy men and women of God, from the time of righteous Abel until now, but, as I look into God's word, and behold the mighty promises of God, and see the miracles which have been wrought on occasions when someone DARED TO BELIEVE, I am persuaded that it REMAINS TO BE SEEN WHAT GOD COULD DO WITH A MAN OR WOMAN WHO WOULD GO ALL THE WAY WITH HIM, and never doubt in their heart! And what immense power would be turned loose against the destroying enemy of mankind -- Satan -- if A GREAT ARMY OF MEN AND WOMEN should all together determine to stand upon God's promises, and believe God for HIS MIRACLE WORKING POWER!

You can be that ONE, or ONE OF THAT GREAT ARMY!

When God looks for a MAN, will you volunteer? WILL YOU BE THAT MAN?

CPSIA information can be obtained
at www.ICGtesting.com
Printed in the USA
BVHW041159050219
539515BV00025B/1728/P